Praise

"Greg serves up an ace with Tennis Doubles Beyon[...]
make you a better doubles player and partner, it wi[...]

Tracy Austin,
Tennis Legend

"While traveling the world playing the great game of doubles, we know fans want to learn more. Mr. Moran has some great ideas and tips on doubles in his new book."

Mike & Bob Bryan,
World #1 Ranked Doubles Team

"Greg Moran has crafted a superb book that cuts to the chase – minimize your errors and construct high-percentage points so your opponents self-destruct. It's a winning strategy that will help players of any level, from club dubs to touring pros. If you take your doubles game seriously, this is a must read."

James Martin,
Editor-in-chief, TENNIS Magazine and TENNIS.com

"Greg has hit a clean winner with Tennis Doubles Beyond Big Shots. His common sense approach to tennis will immediately take your game to the next level."

Tom Gullikson,
Ex-Davis Cup Captain and Olympic coach

"Whether you dream of winning Wimbledon, your league championship or making your school team, Greg's book will help you achieve your goals. Unlike many books out there today, Tennis Doubles Beyond Big Shots reminds us that the mind, not the muscle, is the secret to success. A must read for players who want to win!"

Craig Kardon,
ATP and WTA Tour Coach, Coach of Ana Ivanovic,
Martina Navratilova, Lindsay Davenport

"If you'd like to win more doubles matches this book is for you! Whether you play the game socially or are a serious competitor, Greg's approach and strategic insights will make you a better player and much sought-after partner."

Roy Emerson,
Tennis Legend & 28-time Grand Slam Champion

"Congratulations to Greg Moran for writing a book on the art of doubles. Read up, absorb the knowledge, practice hard, and those close losses will turn around for you."

John Newcombe,
Tennis Legend & 26-time Grand Slam Champion

"Tennis Doubles Beyond Big Shots is a must read for players of all levels. Whether you play socially or are a serious competitor, the strategies and secrets in this book will make you a better player and partner."

Dennis Ralston,
Grand Slam Doubles Champion
and coach of Chris Evert

"To succeed in high level doubles one must be at their peak physically, psychologically and strategically. Greg's latest book will definitely bring out the best in you."

Pat Etcheberry,
Fitness coach to Sampras, Agassi,
Henin and Jankovic

"Greg's approach to the game is strategic, fun and helped my men's 3.5 team win the New England Sectionals."

Arnie Hoegler,
USTA Captain

"Tennis Doubles Beyond Big Shots is a textbook on advanced tennis doubles. Greg's brains over brawn approach made me realize that placement not pace is the secret to success. The information and drills in this book improved my game and will improve yours! "

Bob Griffith,
USTA Competitor

"Greg has convinced us: For winning doubles, playing smart beats hitting big - *and now they've put his secrets in a great book and video combination. "*

Susie & Jim Perakis,
Mixed Doubles Competitors

"Applying Greg's uncanny understanding of tennis and winning doubles strategy greatly improved our USTA match results. A must read for doubles players at all levels. Do your partner a favor, read this book then get him a copy! "

Ann & Gary McManus,
USTA Competitors

An Important Message to Our Readers

This product provides general information and advice in regard to the subject matter covered. It is sold with the understanding that the product does not purport to render medical, legal, and financial or other professional services. If individualized expert advice or assistance is required, the services of a competent professional should be sought.

TENNIS DOUBLES

Beyond

BIG SHOTS

Greg Moran

With Kelley Moran

Mansion Grove House

Tennis Doubles Beyond Big Shots
Copyright © 2009 Greg Moran
Published by Mansion Grove House

ISBN-13: 978-1-932421-20-0   ISBN-10: 1-932421-20-3

Mansion Grove House. Box 201734, Austin, TX 78720 USA.
Website: mansiongrovehouse.com
For information on bulk purchases, custom editions and serial rights:
E-mail sales@mansiongrovehouse.com or write us, Attention: Special Sales
For permission license including reprints, excerpts and quotes: E-mail
permissions@mansiongrovehouse.com or write us, Attention: Permissions

Printed in the United States of America

Library of Congress Cataloging-in-Publication Data

Moran, Greg, 1959-
  Tennis doubles beyond big shots / Greg Moran with Kelley Moran.
     p. cm.
  ISBN 978-1-932421-20-0 (pbk. : alk. paper)
1. Tennis–Doubles. I. Moran, Kelley. II. Title.
  GV1002.8.M67 2009
  796.342'28–dc22
                          2009031521

Tennis Doubles Beyond Big Shots Team!
Designer: Ken Dawes
Illustrator: Christian Kennedy
Video Content: Mike Moran & Tanner Alsop

Credits: See Appendix "Credits"

Contents

To a great team, my parents,

Joy and Stan,

with love and appreciation.

Introduction

In the world of recreational tennis today, doubles is clearly King. Be it competitive teams, leagues or weekly social games, doubles is the game of choice among millions of tennis players around the globe and it's easy to understand why. With its fast-paced exchanges and exciting strategies, high level doubles provides plenty of action, intrigue and a great workout. Plus, it's a lot of fun!

The game also offers a strong sense of camaraderie: there's always someone on the same side of the net to share the highs and the lows. If you're having one of those days where your shots seem to be going everywhere but in the court, your doubles partner is there to pick you up, and vice-versa.

Finally, and perhaps most important, as we get older and may no longer be interested in chasing the ball around the singles court, doubles allows us to still enjoy the game. Every tennis facility in the world has those super seniors, I call them ageless warriors, who have continued to embrace tennis well into their 80s, 90s and beyond. These are my tennis heroes!

Whether you play the game socially, have competitive aspirations or are locked in a three set battle with father time, I'll bet you'd like to take your game to the next level. That's why I wrote this book. "Tennis Doubles Beyond Big Shots" will make you a better doubles player and teammate - **immediately**!

In my last book, "Tennis Beyond Big Shots," I talked about the popularity of what I call "fast food tennis." The secret to success, we're told, lies in developing bigger weapons that will allow us to end points quickly. Big shots are the mark of a winning tennis player and if we can learn to hit the ball lower, at a sharper angle and, of course, **harder**, victory will be ours.

Further feeding our big shot appetites are today's touring professionals. We turn on the television and see Andy Roddick hitting 140 m.p.h serves and Venus Williams firing forehands that would shatter concrete and naturally assume that's what makes them great.

Sure, the pros hit the ball hard, and of course you always want to work on your strokes. However, the key to victory on the pro tour and in the real world of tennis lies not with big shots but rather in developing an understanding of the game.

This book will bring the "Beyond Big Shots" philosophy to doubles. I'm going to strip away the games big shot facade and show you what really happens on the tennis court - the game within the game.

There will be very little technical instruction because you don't need it. You'll learn the pro's secrets to winning doubles and soon discover that your greatest weapon is not the racket you grasp in your hand but rather the knowledge you hold in your mind.

For this book, I teamed up with my favorite partner, on and off the court, my wife Kelley. A former national doubles champion and collegiate Hall of Famer, Kelley has worked with hundreds of doubles players over the past thirty years. As we put this book together, on the court, at the computer and in our living room, Kelley's insights proved invaluable.

As an added bonus, we've included some fabulous tips and drills from many of the world's top teaching professionals. Take their advice, combine it with the information in this book and the companion Video and you'll soon find that you're playing a brand of doubles that will enable you to not only win more matches but have the time of your life doing it!

Greg Moran
Gmfsrc@optimum.net

Tennis Doubles is a Game of .....?

An answer that may surprise you

The world of recreational tennis is filled with players suffering from big-shot envy.

Bob Bryan blasts a serve past his opponent and wins the U.S. Open. Serena Williams puts away a swinging volley and wears an Olympic gold medal. Big serves, huge groundstrokes and the swinging volley are the signature shots of today's champions and tennis players will go to great lengths to emulate their heroes.

Each year, people spend hundreds of hours, and pay well-meaning teaching pros thousands of dollars in an effort to learn to hit the big shots. They feel that if they possess these weapons they'll be able to blow their opponents off the court with a vast array of clean winners.

Sound strategy except for one minor detail - tennis is not a game of winners! Sure, now and then a player will capture a point by hitting a highlight film shot. However, these shots, though phenomenal in their execution, seldom determine who wins or loses the match.

The Secret the Champions Know

The Bryan brothers, Williams sisters and every high level player in the world knows that to win matches they must move beyond simply hitting big shots. These players devise patterns and strategies around the premise that, over and above everything else, tennis is a game of errors!

Studies show that over 80% of the time, at every level of the game, a point ends not with a player hitting a clean winner but rather with one committing an error. What separates the various levels of play are the types of errors that are made.

At the 3.0 level and below, most errors are unforced. It could be that easy volley that we slam into the bottom of the net or a short forehand that we over-hit and deposit into the next county. An unforced error is one that had nothing to do with anything our opponent did. Simply, it's an error we should not have made.

As players improve, groove their strokes and develop an understanding of the game's various strategies, things change. Points still end primarily with someone missing a shot but now more of those errors are forced. For example, you attack the net and your opponent drives a shot down at your feet, forcing you to miss. Or, they serve directly into your body and all you can do is protect yourself. These are errors that are forced by your opponent's strong shot.

So, make no mistake, tennis is a game of errors and successful players have learned to minimize their mistakes and follow a patient, disciplined path to victory.

Unfortunately, in today's "I want it now" world of fast cars, get rich quick schemes and turbo tennis rackets, patience and discipline appear to be largely forgotten. We hear about the "modern game" and are fed catch phrases like: bigger is better, harder will make us happier and hit big to win big. I say that, on the tennis court, bigger is seldom better and that "hit big to win big" more often than not translates into "hit big to lose quickly."

This is particularly true in the game of doubles. There are millions of doubles players around the world who are frustrated with their games. They take lessons, practice, yet their results don't improve. These players walk onto the court, perpetually locked and loaded, and proceed to fire away at the first opportunity. Their points are short, boring and their matches frequently deteriorate into a race to see which team can commit enough errors to lose first.

The Beyond Big Shots philosophy changes all of that. It approaches the game from the perspective of what **really** happens on the tennis court. We're going to teach you how to minimize your errors, construct points and lure your opponents into point-ending mistakes.

As you begin to apply the lessons in this book, your approach to the game and the path of your matches will change dramatically. You'll learn that the key to victory lies not in hitting **better** shots than your opponents but **smarter** shots than your opponents.

It's easier than you think!

1

Find Your Own John McEnroe

Building your dream team

A few years ago, when asked to name the best doubles team in the world, former touring professional Peter Fleming replied, "John McEnroe plus anyone." Fleming was right, McEnroe, with his legendary skill, athleticism and understanding of the game, could play with virtually anyone and be successful. Most of us though, need some help.

There are many ingredients that go into a successful doubles team and choosing a player to share the court with is not a decision to be made quickly. The first step towards building your own dream team is to sit down and take an honest look at your game both physically and mentally. Once you have a firm grasp of your on court strengths and weakness, you can then begin to search for the partner that will help you form a winning combination.

To get started with this self-analysis, ask yourself questions such as:

1. **What are my tennis goals and how much time can I devote to improving my game?**

    Are you primarily a social player? You'd like to improve and compete in the occasional interclub match but with kids, a job and a family to look after, you can only get to the court once a week to practice?

    Or, perhaps the kids are grown, the hectic pace of life has settled down a bit and you now have the time you've always dreamed of to work on your tennis. You're ready to make a serious commitment to improving your game with the ultimate goal being to reach your USTA competitive potential.

    Whichever scenario best describes your current level of commitment, your future doubles partner should share the same.

2. **How effective is my serve: first and second?**

    The serve is the most important shot in the game of doubles and if yours is a weakness, you'd like a partner who's confident and aggressive at the net. By being active up close, they can keep the receiver off balance and take their focus off of your weak delivery. You would also want a strong-serving partner so that your team doesn't present two weak serves to your opponents.

3. **Am I comfortable serving and volleying?**

    If the answer is yes, your partner should be comfortable playing in the both players up formation and also able to anticipate lobs and execute strong overheads. If the answer is no, look for a strong net player who you can set up with your groundstrokes.

4.   **Would I rather hit groundstrokes or volleys?**

If you love to live at the baseline, your partner should be able to end points up at the net. If you prefer to volley your way to victory, find a partner who can join you at the net or set you up with strong groundstrokes.

5.   **How well do I return serve from the deuce and ad courts?**

If your return of serve (the second most important shot in the game) is one of your strengths, you'll want a partner with strong volleys that can pick off the weak shots your aggressive returns will force.

If you struggle to return a big serve, your partner must be comfortable in the hot seat (the service line position). If you have a great return from the deuce court but struggle on the ad side look for a player who prefers the ad court.

7.   **Do I consider myself aggressive or conservative on the court?**

If you're an animal at the net, look for a steady partner who can set you up and also help you weather the inevitable moments of inconsistency that all aggressive players go through. If you're more lamb than lion, find a teammate who loves to be up close and can pick off your opponent's floating shots.

If you don't foam at the mouth when you see a lob coming your way, find a partner that does. It is essential that at least one member of your team loves to see, and can effectively hit, overheads. You should also consider having this player on the ad side so that his strong overhead will be down the center of the court. In a high level doubles match, your team will have to hit lots of overheads. I guarantee it!

Current world champions Bob and Mike Bryan are a great example of a team with a variety of styles. Mike plays a bit more of a steady and conservative game while Bob is the more aggressive of the two. With over 40 pro titles and a career Grand Slam on their resume, I'd say they're a good mix.

9. **Do I tend to get down on myself easily?**

If you're one of those players who see the glass as half empty, find a cheerleader who sees it as half full. Stay away from those who live to lose. These are the self-defeating players who have something negative to say after every point, win or lose. These people can literally suck the life out of you and are no fun to be around on or off the tennis court.

10. **When the big points arrive, do I want the balls to come to me or would I rather they go to my partner?**

If you're not yet comfortable in the pressure situations, find a partner who thrives on the big moment and prefers to play the ad side because that is where many of the big points (40-30 or 30-40) are played.

Be honest with yourself, there are no right or wrong answers. Ask a close friend or your pro to answer the same questions relative to you and your game. Once you consider these questions, you can then begin to intelligently search for a partner who will compliment you technically, tactically and emotionally.

Auditions aren't always Singing and Dancing

Once you know what you're looking for in a partner, the next step is to go where the players hang out and conduct informal auditions. Bob Griffith, a dedicated 4.0 USTA player from Redding CT, has found several long-term doubles partners by attending doubles clinics and social mixers at his club.

"Every player you step onto the court with is a potential partner," says Bob. "As you play with different people, ask yourself if you feel comfortable with their style of play, their personality and mentality. "From there you can put together a list of potential partners, gather a few phone numbers and set up some practice matches. Then, after spending more time on the court together, you can decide who you'd like to team up with."

Setting Your Lineup

After you've found the player to share your doubles journey with, have a team meeting and discuss a few key areas:

· **Who's going to play the deuce court and who's going to play the ad court?**

Many players have strong feelings as to which side of the court they play and draw much of their confidence from that preference.

If your new-found partner **must** play the ad court and that's where you feel most comfortable, you'll have to talk it over. If one of you is not willing or confident enough to make a switch for the good of the team then perhaps you need to reconsider teaming up.

Words From the Wise

USPTA professional and award winning writer, Paul Fein says that "You and your partner should evaluate your strengths, weaknesses and preferences. Your opinions may not coincide, so you have to thrash out any differences.

Some teams have a dominant leader, while others have equal co-captains. Either way, both players must know thy partner as well as know thyself."

A word of advice: if you're one of those players who **must** play a particular side of the court, you're severely limiting the pool of partners from which you could choose. Spend some time playing the other side and I think you'll find that you can become equally comfortable there and actually enjoy the challenge of playing and learning the game from a different perspective.

If neither of you has a strong preference or both are willing to consider changing, the question really boils down to this: each player should play the side where they are most comfortable returning serve. Initially, nothing else matters because if you can't return the serve effectively (away from the net player, down low if the server is coming in, deep if he or she isn't) the point is going to be over faster than a James Blake forehand.

Keep these two statistics in mind:

1. At the 3.5 level and below, most serves are hit to the outside of the service boxes.

2. At the 4.0 level and above, approximately 80 % of serves are hit down the middle.

This means that for a 3.5-and-below-level team of two right-handed players, you would want the player with the stronger forehand returning serve from the deuce court and the player with the better backhand receiving from the ad court.

For teams 4.0 and above, they'll be facing serves coming mostly down the middle, so they would want the player who prefers backhands on the deuce side and the player with the better forehand receiving from the ad court.

Many experts say that the stronger player should play the ad side because that's where most of the "big" points (40-30 and 30-40) in a game occur. This makes sense however if you can't win points from the deuce side, you may never get to the "big" points.

If one member of your team is left-handed then there are other considerations. Some of the greatest doubles teams in history have had the lefty on the ad side. Legendary lefties John McEnroe and Martina Navratilova both played the ad court. The feeling is that the lefty can do real damage on the return of serve from that side as they are often able to move around their backhand and drive a strong, forehand, return of serve.

Plus, McEnroe and Martina are two of the greatest clutch performers in tennis history. Wisely, their partners realized that having them receive serve at 40-30 or 30-40 was in the best interest of the team. Given the fact that they combined to win 248 professional doubles titles (177 for Navratilova and 70 for McEnroe) I'd say that they made the right decision.

Conversely, the Bryan Brothers line up with the lefty, Bob, in the deuce court. Their feeling is that they would prefer to have their strong forehands down the center of the court, where most balls are hit in a high level doubles match.

Again, it boils down to having each player on the side where they are most comfortable receiving serve. Initially, go with this premise and build from there. Remember, once you make your decision, it's only cast in stone for one set. If, after a few matches, you feel it's not working out or your team goes into a slump, switch sides.

Who serves first?

Football, basketball and baseball teams put their strongest lineup on the floor at the start of the game, and so should you. This means that the player who has the best chance of winning their service game should serve first.

Usually this is the player with the more effective serve that can force a weak return. The server, or his partner, can then move forward and attack.

Not always, though. I once had a partner who had a much better serve than I but was also so active and intimidating at the net that we decided it would be better if I served first. I simply spun the serve in and watched my partner dance around the net and drive our opponents crazy.

With his faking, poaching, tremendous foot speed and quick hands, he was able to totally control the point. By putting our best lineup (me serving, he at the net) into the game first, we were able to set an intimidating tone right from the start of the match.

Take a look at both factors: who has the stronger serve and who is more active at the net-and go from there. Keep in mind that the person serving first will have more opportunities to serve during the course of the set, so make sure your starting lineup is a good one.

Note: If you, or your partner, are left-handed, pay close attention to the position of the sun. Quite often, you can you arrange your serving order so that neither of you will have to serve looking into the sun.

Once you've chosen your partner and decided on your starting lineup you'll be well on your way to setting the doubles world on fire.

Doubles Divorce

You've been a team since day one. You bought the same racket at the same time. You took your first lesson together, played your first USTA match as a team and climbed the level ladder simultaneously. You're not only teammates, you're friends which is what makes it all the more sensitive when the time comes to change partners.

People change as do priorities. Relationships grow old and playing with the same person week after week, year after year can get dreary. Plus, you've been putting in extra time at the gym, taking additional lessons and, quite frankly, your game has advanced while your partner's has stagnated.

Doubles teams break up every day. Sometimes, if they're lucky, it's by mutual agreement. For others, the breakup is one sided and that's where it gets tricky. Tim Farwell, Director of Tennis at the Glenview Champions Tennis Club in Florida, says that "Breaking up with your long term doubles partner will never be easy. However, once you have decided that's what you want, you must take immediate action."

"If you delay the breakup," says Tim, "the situation can go from bad to worse. You may, without being aware of it, begin to express your unhappiness with subtle signals and gestures. Your partner will undoubtedly pick up on this and become hurt or upset.

"The best way to divorce your doubles partner and still preserve the friendship is to be straight forward and honest," says Tim. "Tell them the reasons your want a change, thank them for all the good times you've had on the court and wish them the best of luck in the future. Though it will undoubtedly be a difficult conversation to initiate, it's really the only way. Honesty, as always, is the best policy and your ex-partner will eventually appreciate it."

2

Talking Points

The team that babbles the most wins

One of the most enjoyable aspects of doubles is that it's a team game. When you play singles you have to figure things out by yourself. On the doubles court, you have a partner and, as they say, two heads are better than one.

As in any relationship, communication is the key to success. Gary and Ann McManus, who play USTA 8.0 (combined) mixed doubles, say that "as a married couple, effective communication is vital both on and off the doubles court. Positive reinforcement, reviewing successful tactics, and continually assessing opponents' strengths and weaknesses always improve our odds of success. Otherwise, we usually post a loss and have a long car ride home."

Doubles legend, Todd Woodbridge, who captured eleven Grand Slam titles with partner Mark Woodforde agrees. When asked what made the "Woodies" so great, he replied "we communicated very well with each other both on and off the court."

Before you and your new partner step onto the battlefield, sit down and decide how you're going to share your thoughts before, during and after your matches.

Pre-Game Meeting

Communication before your matches should revolve around your upcoming opponents as well as yourselves. The conversation should be both tactical and technical. If you've faced them before, go over the previous match. Go over your opponent's tendencies as well as your team's technique and tactics:

- "Each time Bill served to you on game point, he served out wide."

- "Betty's second serve is really weak so, when she misses her first serve, remember to move forward and jump on her second."

- "John hasn't hit a lob since 1963 so, when we move forward, we can position ourselves right on top of the net."

- "If I start to miss my first serve, remind me to keep my head up."

- "Make sure you're not too aggressive on your first volley. Hit it back cross-court and then we can settle in at the net."

- "We've got to remember to lob when we're in trouble."

If you're facing the other team for the first time and don't know anyone who has played them before, have no fear. Focus on your team's performance. Legendary UCLA basketball coach, John Wooden, did very little scouting of opponents. Wooden felt that if his team focused primarily on exerting maximum effort and running their plays to their best of their ability, the rest would take care of itself.

I'm a big fan of this approach. I'm told that Jimmy Connors rarely scouted opponents and sometimes didn't even know who he was playing until he stepped onto the court. He felt that if he played his game, to his potential, he'd be in good shape.

When facing a team for the first time, focus on playing your game and remind yourselves that you're going to continue to analyze the match as it progresses and discuss potential changes in strategy that might become necessary.

Once You Take the Court

When you're on the court and in the heat of battle, everyone's pumped up and emotions can run high. Communication at this time can be a sensitive issue so be sure to have a predetermined approach for between points and during changeovers.

During points, communication will be at a minimum. Obviously, there will be no extended conversations but as the point progresses there will be many times when a quick, single word of direction is necessary.

For example, when your team is positioned at the net and your opponents throw up a lob, one of you should quickly say "mine" or "me." If you know you have no shot at the ball, say "you." Who covers lobs can be a complicated issue and there are several schools of thought. We'll explore it in depth in a later chapter.

Another situation where a fast word is important would be if you are running down a lob that has gone over your partner's head. A quick "switch" will remind your partner to move to the other side if he hasn't already done so. If you're really struggling to chase down the lob and are certain that you'll hit a weak shot, you want to yell "back" to bring him to the baseline with you.

Balls hit down the middle are one of the most effective shots in the game because they can cause great confusion. I've watched some of the top doubles teams in the world turn and look at each other as the ball travels between them. Here is another situation where a quick word can help. Often the ball is moving too quickly, but if there's time, the player who's closer to the net should call out "mine" and go for it.

Always Keep It Positive

Once a point ends, you have twenty-five seconds to get ready for the next. These few seconds, if used correctly, can be a weapon for your team. This is where you can keep positive momentum flowing and stop negative momentum in its tracks.

High level doubles points can be extremely intense and strenuous so, when the point ends, catch your breath and come down from the stress of the point. As a team, turn away from your opponents walk to the back fence and keep your vision focused on the court.

Your minds will dwell on where your eyes focus so resist the urge to look around. Place your racket in your other hand and look down at your strings. Take 4-5 deep, controlled breaths and, as you push the air out, relax your neck and shoulders. Give yourself 5-10 seconds to recover.

The goal between points is to keep each other pumped up and focused on the match. If your partner has double faulted three times in a row, use this time to help them regain their confidence. If you notice something your opponents are, or are not, doing strategically you can make adjustments.

Once you've caught your breath, use the next 5-10 seconds to re-live the previous point. Observe, without emotion, why you won or lost the point.

Give each other two quick tips and then move on. For example, if your opponents beat you with a lob, remind each other to "look for the lob." If your partner made a tentative forehand error, remind him to "drive through the ball."

Focus on Being a Good Partner

Former British touring pro, Graham Stillwell, says that the importance of being a supportive and helpful partner is vital to the success of all doubles teams.

Graham, who along with fellow countryman Peter Curtis, reached the semi-finals at the 1967 Wimbledon doubles championships says that "Both members of the team should be constantly asking themselves what they can be doing to bring out the best in their partner."

Keep the conversation simple, positive and above all, non-judgmental. Here's my top ten list of things to **never** say to your partner before, during or after a match.

10. "We have to win this one."

9. "How could you miss that shot?"

8. "I could have had that."

7. "Stay on your side."

Words From the Wise

Brad Gilbert former coach of Andre Agassi and Andy Roddick says that "The best doubles teams, like the Bryan twins, Mark Knowles and Daniel Nestor, and Todd Woodbridge and Jonas Bjorkman, are always communicating and setting up plays.

When you design something, such as a serve down the middle to set up a poach, and execute it successfully, it feels great. The positive energy flows within your team."

6. "That's the third overhead in a row you hit onto the next court."

5. "I can't believe we're losing to these guys."

4. "You really stink today."

3. "See if you can hold your serve this time."

2. "I never lost with my last partner."

And, my all-time favorite.......

1. "We're losing because of you."

Believe it or not, I've actually heard players spit out these words to their partners during matches. Aside from being rude, these comments do your partner, and team, no good whatsoever.

Be Aware of Your Body Language

The shoulder slump, the rolling of the eyes, the dropped head and the hands on the hips stance are just a few of the more popular movements insensitive doubles players will make to express their displeasure over an error by their partner.

Nobody tries to miss a shot or blow a point. Negative body language can cut like a knife and take your partner completely out of their game. Plus, when your opponents see this they'll know that there's dissension on your team and that will only pump them up.

Every tennis player has a bad day from time to time. A good partner understands this and realizes that his teammate was not planning to double fault three times each service game or volley into the net on break point. Rather than beat him down further, an experienced partner will do things to pick up his struggling teammate.

The next time your partner makes one of those horrible, unforced, errors at a big moment, use positive body language: stand tall and pick up your shoulders. Walk up to him, gently pat him on the back, pump your fist and, in a positive tone, say things like:

1. "Don't sweat it, we'll get this one."

2. "No problem, let's keep being aggressive."

3. "Come on. We can still come back and win this match."

Using words like "we" and "let's" will show your partner that, even though they may be playing the worst tennis of their life, you're still a team no matter what.

The next time you get a chance to watch the Bryan brothers play you'll notice that they talk after every point. They set up plays, never get down on each other and they keep the energy flowing.

With the remaining few seconds make a plan for the next point. Bounce up and down on your toes. Take a long look at your opponent and give each other a quick tip for your next shot. If you're serving, visualize where you'll place your serve. Say to yourself, "out wide" or "into the body." If you're receiving serve, tell yourself to "focus on the ball and block it back."

The Changeover

During the changeover your team has 90 seconds before the next game begins. Sprint to the sidelines, sit down and towel off your arms, legs and neck. Sip some water, close your eyes and take five deep breaths. Use the first 20 seconds to physically and emotionally recover from the previous two games.

Over the next 45 seconds, take a good look at what's happening in the match thus far. Review the last two games and analyze how your team is winning and losing points. If your opponents are beating you to the net, figure out a strategy to keep them back. If you notice that one of your opponents has a weak overhead, talk about lobbing him.

Also, during this time, sneak a glance at the opposing team. Check out their body language. Do they appear tired, frustrated or angry? If they're arguing, that's a good sign for your team. It means that you're obviously getting to them so stick with the game plan you've been using.

Pick Up on Their Tactics

Most players will hit the same shot again and again in a given situation so remind yourself of your opponent's tendencies. Where do they serve on big points? When you attack the net on your opponent's deuce side, does the player try to pass you cross-court or does he go for the big shot down the alley? Identifying and planning for to these tendencies can often win you the match.

I saw a great example of this recently when Arnie and Roger played in a big USTA match. Throughout the match, they had paid strict attention to the opposing team's tendencies and noticed two things:

1. That on big points, one of their opponent's, John, always served out wide.

2. When under pressure, Frank (John's partner) tended to panic and would try to rip a winner down the alley.

When the third set tiebreaker reached six points all, John was preparing to serve to Arnie. Roger immediately reminded his partner of John's tendency to serve out wide on the big points. As John released his toss, Arnie shifted out wide, began to prepare his racket and, sure enough, the serve came right to him—just as expected. Arnie was then able to drive a low return of serve at John's feet for the mini-break.

On the next point, match point for Arnie and Roger, Frank was set to return serve. Roger was playing the net and Arnie reminded him of Frank's tendency to go for the alley. Just before Frank hit his return of serve, Roger shifted over towards his alley.

Staying true to form, Frank went for the big shot down the alley. Roger could barely conceal his smile as he easily volleyed the ball away to capture the match. These small pieces of information, that Arnie and Roger had picked up during the match and actually written down during a changeover, proved to be invaluable when the match was on the line.

With the remaining few seconds, plan your team's strategy for the next two games. If you're winning the match, don't change a thing. "Never change a winning game" as the legendary Bill Tilden once said.

Be sure to avoid the all too common trap of complacency. I've lost count of the number of times a team has come up to me after a loss, complaining that, "we won the first set and were rolling. Then, it all got away from us. We don't know what happened."

What happened, in all probability, was that once the team got ahead, they suffered a letdown. Relieved that they won the first set, their focus drifted. They lost a few points in a row, then a few games and then it all snowballed. Before they knew it, they were shaking hands at the net on the wrong end of the score.

Once your team takes the lead, keep the pedal to the metal. Be ready for an increased effort from your opponents as they'll fight hard to change the momentum of the match. To ward off that inevitable surge, focus your efforts towards winning the first two games of the next set. Strive to get up 30-love in each game and keep each other pumped up between points and during changeovers.

If your team is comfortably ahead or the match is close, stick with your game plan. Bounce up out of your chair and be the first back on the court. Let your opponents see that you're eager to play.

If your team finds itself slightly behind, don't panic. Close matches are usually won and lost by a few points. Stick with your game plan. If you can win a few of the big points, you can easily turn the match around.

If your team is getting blown off the court, slow the pace of the match down. Use every one of your 90 seconds. Let your opponents walk back onto the court first. Make them play to your pace. Once play resumes, use the full 25 seconds between points.

Just because your opponents may be on a roll for the first few games of the match, it doesn't mean that they can keep it up for two or three sets. By making them play to your team's pace, within the rules of course, you can often take them out of their rhythm and turn the match around.

At least seventy-five percent of a tennis match is spent in between points and during changeovers. By learning to control this game within the game you'll most likely be the team smiling at the end of the match.

3

One Step to the Advanced Level

Your most important move in the game

Before we take to the court, there is one secret that I must pass along to you. It has absolutely nothing to do with how you hold or swing your racket yet is one of the most important techniques in the game. Tennis legend Stefan Edberg says that "everyone can hit the ball out there but getting to it and getting to the right place at the right time is really what tennis is all about." Edberg's right. Your strokes are largely dictated by how well you move your feet. When the time comes to swing your racket, you can only move your shoulders, hips, arms and legs in a manner which your body will allow.

If you're well positioned and balanced, you'll be able to execute a smooth, controlled stroke, if not, your stroke will likely breakdown.

You'll struggle to control your shot and potentially injure yourself.

Proper positioning, which is an essential to stroke production, begins with a quick start. This is particularly true in the world of doubles which, at the higher levels, is an exceptionally fast moving game.

Every Good Player Does This

The next time you get a chance to watch the pros, or even the best players at your club, focus solely on their feet. Aside from the fact that their feet are almost always in motion, you'll notice that, every now and then, they take a small hop up into the air. Then, as they land, they immediately explode off in the direction of the ball, execute a smooth stroke and, as we so often hear, "make it look so easy." This small hop is known as a split-step and when mastered, will take your game to the next level immediately!

The secret to a winning split-step lies in the timing. If you hop too soon, you'll be off balance when your opponent strikes their shot. If you're late, you'll be slow reacting. As your opponent prepares to hit their next shot, pay close attention to their racket. As it begins to move forward towards the ball, bend your knees and take a short hop (no more than a few inches off the court).

Time the hop so that you are in the air as the ball is struck. As you come down, and have determined which way the ball is traveling, touch down first with your outside foot (the foot furthest away from the oncoming ball). Then, with an explosive push, turn your body towards the ball and begin moving.

For example, if you're a right handed player and, during your split-step, you notice the ball coming to your forehand side, your left foot (outside) would touch down just before your right (inside) and then push you off towards the ball.

Though you may find the timing a bit difficult at first, keep working on it and, in a short while, you'll find that you're reacting significantly faster and feel as if you have all day to prepare for your shot.

The next time you take the court, commit to taking a split step before every shot your opponent (or practice partner) hits. I like to have my students actually say the word "split" at the appropriate time to remind them to use the split step.

In addition to helping you react to shots quicker, the split step will help you stay mentally alert. I often find that when my feet get lazy, my mind wanders. When I remind myself to get up on my toes and take strong split-steps, my focus, and level of play improve dramatically.

By the way, many players associate the split step only with an approach to the net. The truth is you and your partner should split step every single time your opponents prepare to strike the ball.

Keri Blank, a Pat Etcheberry certified trainer in West Virginia says that, "during the course of a typical tennis match you'll hit hundreds of balls. If you're going to split step before every shot, not to mention move quickly and efficiently around the court, you'll need to develop strong and flexible leg muscles."

Here are two exercises that Keri recommends to target the key quadriceps and calf muscles:

Active Squats: Grab your tennis racket and assume the ready position: feet, a shoulders width apart, knees slightly bent, and hold your racket at approximately waist height. From that position, bend your knees until you feel tension come into your quads. Hold that position for a five count and then rise back up. Be sure to keep your back straight and make certain that your knees do not extend out over your feet. Repeat 10 times. Build up to three sets of 15.

Racket Jumps: Place your racket horizontally on the court in front of you. Stand behind the grip with your feet approximately 2-3 inches apart. Using your quads and then calves, bend down approximately 2-3 inches and hop over the racket and then back, springing as you go. As you want to train your body for what it will face on the court, remember that the average tennis point lasts for less than ten seconds. So begin by doing one, 10-second, set of racket jumps. As you get stronger, increase the number of sets that you do.

Try these exercises, commit to mastering the split step and you'll notice a new spring in your step on the court. Plus, as you develop a quicker first step, you'll find that you'll not only get to more balls but the quality of all your shots will rise.

4

Ladies and Gentlemen, Start Your Engines

How to control the net

When you watch doubles played at the 4.0 level and above you'll frequently see four players up close intensely battling it out: reflex volleys exchanged at a dizzying pace with each team stretching, straining and striving to inch closer and closer to the net. These players know that the team that controls the net controls the point. In fact, tennis legend, and ten-time Grand Slam doubles champion Anne Smith, estimates that "the team that controls the net first in doubles wins the point an amazing 85% of the time." That being the case, high level doubles can best be described as a race - a race to the net.

If you and your partner can win that race, you'll have several advantages over your opponents:

- From a visual standpoint, as you move forward, the net will seem lower and the court larger. The next time you step onto the court, stand on your baseline and look at your opponent's court. You'll find that the majority of their court appears below the net. Now, as you walk forward, you'll see that the net, slowly but surely, moves below your line of vision and your opponent's court becomes much clearer. Both can be huge psychological pump-ups.

- Technically, it's much easier to hit a volley than it is a ground stroke. Groundstrokes require more preparation, longer swings and intense movement and timing. Volleys, for the most part only demand that, from the ready position, you turn your shoulders, move 1-2 steps and then push the racket forward with little or no follow-through. If a high level baseliner and net player get into a groundstroke/volley exchange, more often than not the baseliner will miss first. They're working harder to generate their groundstrokes than the net player is to execute their volleys.

- From a strategic standpoint, one of your primary goals is to force your opponents to pop the ball "up" so that you can then aggressively drive it back "down." This means that, at the appropriate time, your team can end the point either by drilling a volley down at your opponent's feet, hitting down the middle, or angling the ball off to the side. You can't drive "down" from the baseline, only at the net.

- Each time your team takes the net, you put a tremendous amount of pressure on the opposing team. Your shots will appear to have more pace and your opponents will be forced to come up with a good return each time they strike the ball. If they don't, your team is in position to end the point with one shot.

When your team takes the net, your opponents have few options at their disposal. Experienced teams have learned to constantly move together as the ball travels back and forth across the net. By doing so, they cover the majority of the court, leaving their opponents with very few escape routes.

Imagine that you're playing doubles against the club champions, Bill and Sam. In the diagram here, you're positioned on the deuce side of the court and your opponents have won the race to the net. The ball has come wide to your forehand and you move to your right, preparing to hit your shot.

As you're moving, Bill and Sam, being the champions that they are, **immediately** shift to their left. Bill moves directly in front of you, covering your shot down the line towards his alley (1) and two or three feet to his right (2). Sam moves to cover the middle (3) and two or three feet to his right (4). Here's what you will be looking at as you prepare to hit your shot:

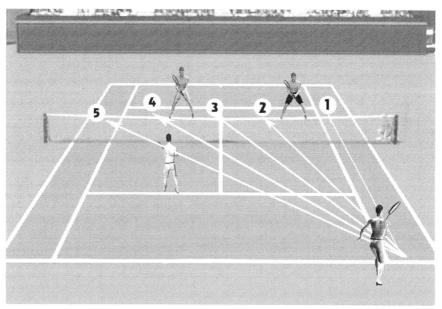

What are you going to do? Under this type of pressure you have basically two choices: execute an extremely low ground stroke or a very good lob. Sure, you could try a sharply angled cross-court return past Sam (5). However, that's the most difficult spot for you to place the ball from where you're positioned.

Is this shot make-able? About 10% of the time for most players and believe me, your opponents will like nothing more than for you to be trying to hit clean, angled winners past them when they are properly positioned at the net. They know that this approach will result in far more errors than winners.

High level doubles team have mastered the art of shifting side to side and positioning themselves so that the only "open" space they leave their opponents is the area of the court that's most difficult to hit. So, the ultimate goal for your team is to control the net. However, there is a catch.

To be effective up close, both you and your partner must be able to volley well, move properly and anticipate and reply to lobs from your opponent. These are skills that take a while to develop and your current level of play will pretty much dictate how successful your forays to the net will be.

If you are a beginner up to a 3.0 level player, you may initially struggle when you venture into the land of fast feet, quick volleys and deep overheads. This is why you see so many recreational players in the traditional one up and one back formation.

These players have not yet developed the techniques needed for success at the net. As a result, their points usually go like this: two players exchanging groundstrokes while their partners stand at the net watching, hoping that the ball will eventually come to them - or that it doesn't.

The only time either team has both players at the net is when one baseline player is forced forward to retrieve a short shot. Then, suffering from a serious case of net-phobia, that player scrambles back and continues the baseline rally. "We've got it all covered," they say to me. "I take the backcourt, Betty plays the net and we're good to go." Well, they may be good to go and enjoy their tennis tremendously but if they aspire to upper level tennis, they'll find this approach a tough path to take.

Of the three basic formations at each team's disposal (one up and one back, two at the net or two at the baseline) this popular positioning is the most difficult to be successful from, particularly when your opponents take the net.

As you can see in the diagram below, the team in the one up one back formation is at a huge disadvantage. First, there's a huge gap between the two players into which their opponents can hit (1) plus, the single player at the net becomes a sitting duck (2) for a strong volley.

If the other team wins the sprint to the net, you'll frequently be better off moving both players back to the baseline. Though it is generally a defensive position, you won't give your opponents a mid-court target and you'll be surprised how long you can stay in, and often turn around, points by mixing up drives and lobs. We'll take a look at both the one up, one back and both back formations, in a later chapter.

For success at the 4.0 level and beyond, you need to be comfortable coming to the net. I frequently tell the story of Rick, a 3.0 level player, who wanted to improve his doubles. Like all good students, Rick had taken his pros advice and begun to work on his net game.

After a few lessons focusing on volleys, overheads, movement and net strategy Rick felt he was ready to rumble. He turned up for his regular Saturday morning doubles match with his buddies ready to attack the net at the first opportunity.

The following week, Rick appeared for his lesson wearing a chest protector and batting helmet. The first words out of his mouth were, "I thought you said that the team that gets to the net first controls the point." Rick was shell-shocked. He'd made his way to the net and found that things happen much faster up close where the strong players hang out.

We can all sympathize with Rick. The net can be a frightening place. When you and your partner venture forward, you're much closer to your opponent and the ball's coming at you twice as fast. Plus, there's the ever present fear of being lobbed.

"Every time I come to the net, they lob over our heads so I'm not coming in," is a comment every teaching pro in the world hears on a regular basis. Their frustration is understandable because though the strategy is simple, the execution is not.

You cannot recklessly charge the net and expect your opponent's to wilt under the mere pressure of your presence. You need to learn when to come in, how to come in and what to do once you are in.

When Should I Come In?

As soon as you possibly can!

The partners of the server and receiver have a head start in their journey to the net: the server's partner is already there and the receiver's partner, positioned at the service line, is close and, if his partner hits a strong return, ready to move forward and pounce. So, the prize of controlling the net frequently breaks down to a race between the server and the receiver with the server having a decided advantage. I'll discuss the strategy for both these positions in a later chapter.

Words From the Wise

To help his doubles players develop the all-important instinct of moving forward, USPTA Master Professional Feisal Hassan, has them play Inside Doubles. Here's how it works.

"Play doubles but the only rule is that the players must physically stay within the lines of the court. You cannot step behind the baseline or outside of the doubles alley line. If you do your team automatically loses the point. This will force you to think 'move forward,' a key ingredient for winning doubles.'"

5

No Fear

Mastering the close-up game

Controlling the net is the goal but whether you're following your serve to the net, advancing behind a strong return or sneaking in behind a lob, moving forward can be as frightening as a midnight stroll down a dark alley.

It's the fear of the unknown and it's perfectly natural. You don't know if your opponent is going to try to pass you to the left or to the right. Maybe they'll drill the ball right at you or, God forbid, they throw up a lob.

When I watch recreational players move towards the net, I always look into their eyes. Sometimes I see determination. Frequently though, I see fear because they really don't want to be coming to the net and are doing so only because their pro told them to.

Moving forward can be a scary proposition but by following a few simple strategies, you can learn to not only love the net but, in the process, watch your team's number of wins skyrocket.

Once your team gains control of the net your success will largely be determined by how well you:

· Move Together

· Anticipate Drives & Lobs

· Execute Volleys & Overheads

Follow the Ball

Mike Bryan says that "the key to doubles is moving together" and with a house full of doubles championships, when Mike talks, we should listen. Movement at the net entails two facets: side to side and up or back.

The first rule of doubles net play says to follow the ball from side to side. This allows your team to cover the majority of your opponent's likely shots. If the ball goes to the right, your team moves to the right. See below.

The player on the deuce side, Chris, covers shots hit down his alley (1) as well as 1-2 steps to his left (2). The ad-court player, Milton, will cover balls hit down the middle (3) as well as shots 1-2 steps to his left (4). The only "open space" is a sharply angled ball to the left side of Milton (5).

If their opponents hit the clean winner to the #5 area, Chris and Milton will simply say "too good" and move onto the next point. They know that it's unlikely their opponents will be able to execute that low percentage shot consistently throughout the match.

If the ball goes to the left, Chris and Milton should shift as well.

Now, Milton covers his alley as well as two or three feet to his right (1 & 2). Chris will cover balls hit towards the middle (3) as well as shots two or three feet to his right (4). The only "open space" is then a sharply angled ball to Chris's right side (5).

If the ball goes down the middle, you'll see that both Chris and Milton will take a step towards the center. From this positioning, they'll only be leaving sharp angles on each side open (1& 2) open. If their opponents return the ball down the center, the player closer to the net will hit it.

The key is that both players must move together. If you follow the ball and your partner stays still, you'll leave a huge gap down the middle of the court for your opponents to hit through.

Since most shots (over 75%) in high level doubles are hit down the center, it's vital that you and your partner move together to keep the middle properly covered. One of the great all-time tennis tips is for doubles teams to imagine that each player has an eight foot rope tied around their waist. When one player moves, the other must follow.

To practice this vital movement, grab your doubles partner, a friend, a basket of balls and head to the practice court. You and your partner position yourselves at the net with your friend (and the basket of balls) behind you. Have your buddy slowly hit balls to the other side of the net, first to the left and then the right. You and your partner practice moving side to side, together, following the ball.

After a while, have him speed up his feeds so you'll have to quicken your movement. Finally, have him randomly feed side to side so that your team will be forced to read and adjust to each shot. After a few minutes, rotate positions so that everyone gets to feed and practice this all-important doubles movement.

What are They Going to Do?

Once you've got the court covered laterally, you must next answer the most important question every team faces when they play the net: are your opponents going to lob or drive their shot? I tell my players that if they get this right, they can make the rest up as they go. Of course, an exaggeration, but it gets them thinking.

As your team moves laterally to follow the ball, you'll also need to move up or back depending upon whether you anticipate a lob or a drive. When you learn to read the signals you can answer this question correctly most of the time!

Common tennis wisdom tells us to watch our opponent's racket to get a feel for what they're going to do with their shot. While this is certainly sound advice, I feel that the anticipation process can begin long before your opponent even begins their racket preparation. It begins when the ball leaves your racket.

After you strike your shot, pay attention to how it feels coming off your strings. You can feel it when you've hit a strong shot and you know when you've hit a weak one. Next, notice how your opponent's react. Watch their body. If they're comfortably moving forward as they approach the ball my first instinct tells me that they're probably going to drive their shot. It takes a very skilled player to execute a lob as they're running forward and most players innately want to drive the ball. Moving forward encourages them to do so.

Next, look at their racket face. If it's flat or slightly closed (strings pointing down to the court), they've virtually committed to the drive so you should immediately take two quick steps forward and prepare to volley as Chris and Milton have done below. Split step just before they make contact and then attack the volley with quick feet and a short motion.

Here are a few more tips to keep your volleys sharp:

· If you're not already, become comfortable with the continental grip. It's the best grip for volleying, hands down.

· Always keep your hands up at chest height and, after each volley, immediately bring them back up.

· Keep your feet active and always split step before your opponent strikes the ball.

· Once you see the volley coming, immediately push forward toward the net. Go to the ball. Don't wait for it to come to you.

· Stay away from the swinging volley - for most players, it's a reckless, impatient shot.

Quick hands and a short motion are two of the keys to winning volleys. Here are two drills that the Bryan brothers have done since their junior days.

Words From the Wise

Paul Annacone, former coach of Pete Sampras, says that "When it comes to volleying, less is more. You want as little motion with your racket and body as possible. Big swings and lots of movement lead to inconsistent results."

Lateral Drill

Line up on one service line and have your partner line up on the other as pictured below. Feed the ball in play and volley back and forth as you both move across the service line, crossing in front of each other, on your way to the other end. Go back and forth as many times as you can, picking up the pace of your shots as you improve.

Closing Drill

Line up as pictured below. Feed the ball in play and then both players immediately begin moving forward. As you and your partner volley back and forth, keep moving forward towards the net. As you get closer and closer the pace will pick up and you'll be forced to speed up your reflexes.

Both of these drills are fabulous for quickening your hands and feet as well as shortening your volley motion. They've obviously served the Bryans well.

Here's one more for you: The next time you and your partner go out to practice, start on opposite sides of the net, in the middle of each service box, facing each other. Put a ball in play and volley back and forth at a comfortable pace.

Once you develop a rhythm and are volleying back and forth, feed in a second ball and try to keep both going. This will not only quicken up your hands but also speed up your eyes, both vital elements for successful volleys.

Conquering "Lob-itis"

Many players fear being lobbed and that fear is well founded. No shot in the game changes the complexion, forces more errors, and wins more points than a well struck lob. If you're one of those players suffering from chronic lob-itis, have no fear: with a few simple steps you can learn to turn your opponent's lob into a weapon for your team!

Again, it begins with anticipation. When your shot has your opponent scrambling backwards or to the side, the lob alert should go off in your head. If you notice them leaning back and their racket face is open (strings pointing toward the sky), a lob is not far behind so quickly back up.

As you can see below, Chris and Milton see that their opponent is deep in his backcourt and anticipate a lob. They both move back, positioning themselves near the service line, before the ball is struck. From this position, there'll be no lob they can't handle.

Once the lob goes up, the first task is to determine which member of the team is going to deal with it. We've all the heard the old joke: "What is the most common word in the game of doubles?" The punch line, of course is "Yours!"

Though there are several schools of thought on this, among high level players the first rule of lob coverage is:

If the lob is on your side of the court it's yours!

Strong, confident players want the ball so that when that lobs goes up, your first thought should be, "Great, an overhead smash!"

Immediately push your left foot into the court and swing your right leg back. Turn your shoulders and hips in the same direction while also bringing your racket straight up past your right ear (much like when you pick up a telephone) and place it into the "backscratch" position.

As your right arm moves behind your head, place your left index finger up and point at the oncoming ball. This will help you to track the ball and position yourself accordingly using either shuffle or crossover steps. Do not run backwards, you might fall.

Words From the Wise

To ensure a proper shoulder turn on overhead smashes, USPTA & PTR professional Geoff Norton tells his students to "point at the ball with their non-racket elbow."

If your index finger is falling in front of you, it means that the lob is short. Move in towards the net, hit a strong overhead, and end the point.

If you notice that your non-racket arm is moving back over your head and you're forced to move backwards, you now have another decision to make.

Many players, at the 3.5 level and below, find that it works best for their team if their partner covers their lobs and vice versa. There is validity to this approach: moving backwards for a lob requires a great deal of agility and coordination. Players, who have not yet developed these skills, feel that their partner will have an easier angle to get to the shot. They're correct except the plan has a few flaws:

1. The crossing partner has to move a longer distance to reach the ball.

2. Most of the time, the crossing player will have to let the ball bounce which means that their opponents will be able to charge, and take over control of, the net.

I'm not a big fan of this approach because I feel it gives the player who's been lobbed an easy safety net. I'll never forget the time I was giving a ladies clinic to Susie and Anne. During the course of a point, they both had advanced to the net and were waiting for their opponents to hit their shot.

The shot came and it was a lob over Susie. She immediately put her head down and switched sides, expecting Anne to cross and cover the lob. When the ball bounced, it landed about six inches behind where Susie started. If she'd stayed still the ball probably would have hit her in the head.

Susie had become so conditioned to immediately switching and letting her partner cover her lobs that she never gave hitting the ball herself a thought. That's why I discourage this strategy with my students - I feel that it dissuades the person who's been lobbed from going for the ball.

That being said, there are instances when your team will have to use the switch and cover approach. For example, if you and your partner are both at the net and you're drawn in close for a low volley.

As you move forward, your partner, anticipating a possible lob on your opponent's next shot, should take a few steps back. When that lob comes, he can easily move over and handle it. You can then switch sides and stay in the point. This is one of the few situations where you and your partner would not move together.

Blast, Bunt or Bounce

Your ultimate goal with every lob is to hit the ball before it bounces. If you let the ball bounce behind you, more often than not you'll put your team on the defensive and your opponent will move in and take control of the net and the point.

An exception to this would be if you're playing outside and your opponent hits a high, defensive lob into the stratosphere. The higher the lob, the faster it falls and the more difficult it is for you to time.

The "moonball" lob will still bounce up high enough for you to hit an aggressive overhead. Also, if you're looking into the sun, you may want to let the ball bounce to give you a bit more time to prepare. Be sure to use you left hand to shield your eyes from the sun.

As you move into position, you must make an important decision: blast or bunt. If you can get back quickly and balance yourself behind the ball, go for the blast - a strong overhead smash either down the middle or at the opposing net player's feet. As you prepare for your overhead, keep these few tips in mind:

- Get behind the ball so that, as you swing you can move back into it.

- Time your swing so that you contact the ball with your arm extended.

- Be sure to keep your head up through the shot.

- As you make contact, snap your wrist down so that your racket face is square to the ball at impact. Note: if you're using a continental grip (as you should) you'll need to pronate your wrist to get solid contact.

If you're struggling to hit a balanced overhead, or are forced to play the ball on your backhand side, simply turn the shot into a high volley. Take the ball out of the air and use a short motion as if you were giving your opponent a "high five." Bunt the ball back deep, maintain control of the net and begin to anticipate the next shot.

Worst Case Scenario

While the goal is to hit your opponent's shot before it bounces, there will be times when a lob is just too good for you to take out of the air. In this case, run back as quickly as you can and try to get behind the ball. Don't run directly at the ball but rather, circle around it.

As you're moving back, briefly move your eyes away from the ball and take a quick look at your opponents. If they stay in the backcourt there's no real pressure on you.

Simply lob the ball back, move into position for a baseline rally and try to get back to the net as quickly as possible.

Much more likely, you'll be faced with two players charging the net, eager to move in for the kill. Now you have to come up with something good. More often than not, this should be another lob.

It amazes me how often I see players, trapped off balance six feet behind the baseline, with the ball on top of them try to rip a winning passing shot. Perhaps this is a good play if your name is Federer, Williams or your dad is Wayne Bryan but for most of us, it's a low percentage play.

If you can get back in time to set up behind the ball, you can consider driving a low return but, if you feel off balance in any way, throw up a lob, keep it deep and make your opponents deal with the physically demanding overhead. Remember, you always want to give your opponent the opportunity to hand you the point with an error.

Words From the Wise

Tom Gullikson, who has coached Pete Sampras & Andre Agassi, says that a "common error among recreational players is that they drop their heads as they hit their overhead."

"By thinking of a third eye on your chin, it will help you to keep your head up towards the sky and improve your overhead dramatically."

Move Your Feet and Open your Mind

Once your team takes control of the net, keep your feet active. Move side to side and up or back every time the ball crosses the net. Ask yourself that key question as your opponents prepare to strike the ball: lob or drive?

Remember, if your opponent is moving forward they're probably going to hit a drive. If they're backing up, look for a lob.

If you're not sure, guess lob. If you anticipate a lob, move back and you're wrong, you'll still have a play at your opponent's drive as it moves at or past you. However, if you keep charging and your opponent lobs, you'll be stuck as the ball floats over your head.

Here's a fabulous drill from one of the game's all-time greats, Brian Gottfried, designed to help you work on your volley consistency and overhead control:

"Being able to make the transition back and forth between volleys and overheads is one of the key ingredients of a winning doubles player," says Gottfried, who won 54 doubles titles, including Wimbledon and the French Open during his career. "When you and your partner take to the practice court, give this drill a try and I think you'll find that your transition game will improve dramatically."

One player positions himself at the center of the net. The other player will position himself on the other side of the court, at the baseline, in one corner or the other. The player at the baseline starts the rally and the net player must volley back to the same corner until the baseline player throws up a lob.

When the lob is in the air, the baseline player calls out where he wants the overhead to be hit: forehand, backhand or middle. He then shifts to that spot. The net player hits the overhead to the designated area with pace and then the point is played in the singles court. Play a game to 11. The baseline player can alternate corners after each point is played.

Make a vow to control the net and remember, a lob from your opponent should not be feared. As you learn to open your mind, and read the signs, you and your partner will ultimately come to view the once dreaded lob as a point ending gift.

6

Get It Over With? No Way

Easy ways to an effective serve

Doubles matches at the advanced level are often decided by a single service break each set. If your team never loses serve, you'll seldom lose a match. It's that simple and with the right approach you can make that happen.

It All Begins With the Server

It is tempting for players to frequently view the serve as little more than an annoying way to begin the point: push it in and let's get on with it. In fact, I often see 2.0-3.0 level doubles players actually beg to serve first just so they "can get it over with."

These are the same players who often employ the "grip it and rip it" approach. They hit the first serve as hard as they possibly can, hope it will go in (and not hit their partner in the back of the head) and give their team an easy point. It's a no-brainer strategy in their mind because they know that if it doesn't go in (which is usually the case) they can always push in their second serve and still be in the point.

Players at this stage have yet to learn the importance of the serve and have spent the majority of their practice time working on their baseline and net games. As a result, there are a lot of recreational players out there who may be 3.5-4.0 level players in every aspect of their games, except their serves. When they attempt to play in 4.0 level leagues or tournaments, they'll find that their lack of an effective serve will hurt their team big time!

On the other side, I have a student who is a solid 3.5 level player but, through patience and practice, has developed a 4.5 quality serve. Because of this, his serve is actually a level above the rest of his game and allows him to hold his own in doubles matches with players who, for the most part, are at a higher level.

Educated players know that the serve is the most important part of the game and have put their time into developing one that is truly a weapon. As you develop your serve keep these two goals in mind:

- You must be confident that you can put the ball in play on a consistent basis.

- You must be able to get your opponent off-balance in some way. More often than not, that doesn't mean power.

Yes, blasting a big serve is one way to hurt your opponents and make you feel good but, it's rarely the best approach. Hard, flat serves have little margin for error and you'll probably miss more than you make. This leaves your opponents foaming at the mouth as they wait for your second serve. Plus, if you're serving and volleying, the harder you hit your serve, the faster it's going to come back, giving you less time to move in and prepare to volley.

Unless you can consistently hit your serve in the court at over 100 mph, you're better off thinking spin and placement. That's why you see a large number of players hitting a 3/4 pace serve with lots of spin on their first serves. A spin serve moves slower through the air than a flat serve, which will give you more time to move to the net. Your ultimate goal should be to hit an effective serve that allows you to move up, join your partner at the net and take control of the point.

If your serve is not quite up to par with the rest of the game, here are a few goals to work towards that will bring your delivery to the next level.

1. **Develop a consistent toss.** Initially, nothing else matters. Many players, out of frustration will adjust their swing to accommodate an erratic toss while it should be the other way around. Here are two classic reminders to help you groove your toss:

    · Imagine balancing a glass of water in the palm of your hand as you release the ball. This will help you place the ball out in front of your body.

    · Try to release the ball into the air without it spinning. This will help you to cut down on any wrist flick or finger roll that can throw your toss off its course.

2. **Become comfortable serving with the continental grip.** It puts the racket at an angle in your hand which, depending upon how you swing your arm and snap your wrist, enables you to hit flat, slice and topspin serves. You may struggle for a while and be tempted to go back to you old reliable grip but if you can persevere, your serve will become a true weapon.

Words From the Wise

To cure an inconsistent toss, USPTA Master Pro Ajay Pant, suggests changing the terminology. "Tossing is not usually associated with a smooth and controlled action. You toss a football or basketball, and use your arm, wrist and elbow to do it. But when we ask a student to toss a tennis ball, what we are really asking him to do is "place" the ball. There is no "toss."

'Place' the ball more accurately defines what the tossing arm is meant to do. The arm simply lifts and releases the ball when the arm is fully extended. The fingers, wrist and elbow do not move. So remember, "place" the ball for a better serve."

Once you master the continental grip, here are a few reminders for hitting the various serves:

- **Flat**: Toss the ball 1-2 feet in front of your body at approximately 1 o'clock (12 o'clock is directly in front of you). As you reach up and out to make contact, pronate (turn) your wrist so that your palm is facing the net at impact. Make contact with your arm fully extended and follow through to the left side of your body.

- **Slice**: Same toss as for the flat serve, except now, as you swing the racket, imagine the ball as the face of the clock. Make contact at 3:00 and, using your arm and wrist, swing around, right to left, as if you're peeling an orange.

- **Topspin**: Toss the ball at 12 o'clock and slightly behind your body. Again, see the ball as the face of a clock and swing up and out from 7:00-1:00.

3. **Develop control & consistency to different areas of both service boxes**. Set up targets and practice aiming for them. Pick various spots along the baseline and practice serving to different areas of the service box. Choose a spot close to the center line, another mid way between the center line and sideline and a third close to the sideline.

When you serve from these three points, it will change the angle that your serve moves towards your opponent, making it more awkward for them to return.

Now, choose three areas within each service box: out wide, down the center and down the middle. If you can develop topspin and slice

Words From the Wise

To help players learn to use their wrist when they serve, Rick Macci suggests serving while holding the racket with just your thumb and index finger.

Macci, whose students have included Andy Roddick and Venus Williams, says that by doing this, "you're allowing the racket to move naturally and do the work instead of muscling the ball. The wrist is more playful and snaps the racket through contact."

serve to all three areas of the service box from three different spots along the baseline, you'll have eighteen different serves to throw at your opponent. Plus, if you can throw in the occasional flat serve to all three spots, from all three areas of the baseline, you'll have 27 different serves at your disposal.

Be sure to spend extra time working on serving to the "T" as well as into the body of your opponent. This is where at least 75% of your serves should be hit during your matches.

Develop a Serving Ritual

As you prepare to serve, it's vital that you relax and clear your head. The best way to achieve this calm state is to develop a serving ritual. A serving ritual is a series of movements that you go through before every point to get yourself in the proper, focused, frame of mind. It can be as simple as bouncing the ball, adjusting your cap like Jim Courier or taking several deep breaths. On big points, Novak Djokovic will often bounce the ball 15-20 times to help himself get centered.

Develop your own ritual and use it before every serve. If you're tense or it's a big point, go through your ritual twice. It will help you put your mind and body in sync and allow you to focus on hitting your best serve.

Developing a top level serve does not have to be boring. Come to the practice court with your doubles partner and practice hitting targets. Make it fun and competitive. Keep score and the player who hits the fewest targets buys lunch.

Believe me, the time spent developing your serve will pay off in a major way in your matches. Once you and your partner have developed solid first and second serves, a whole new set of strategies will be at your team's disposal.

Using your Weapon

Your top priority with each point is to get your first serve in. When you do, you'll have the receiver off balance because they don't know what to expect in terms of placement, spin or speed. They'll have to react very quickly to the serve and hope to hit a reasonable return.

If you miss your first serve, you've forfeited a big part of that advantage. The receiver knows that you're under pressure to get your next serve in and, as a result can expect a weaker delivery. This means that he can attack his return. That's why you'll frequently see the receiver move forward after the server has missed his first serve: he's preparing to attack.

So, when serving, your first goal is to get that first serve in. The Bryan brothers strive to get their first serves in 70% of the time. Your team should as well. The late Arthur Ashe had a great rule of thumb when serving. If Arthur missed his first serve on two successive points, he would hit his second serve first, on the third point. This was a great strategy for Arthur, a true legend on and off the court, and it can be for you as well.

From a purely percentage basis, most serves should be hit down the middle of the court. This placement makes it difficult for your opponent to return down the line, past your partner at the net, it reduces the angles that he has at his disposal plus it sets your partner up for a poach.

Keep in mind that percentages are merely strategies to be employed when all things are equal. If you notice that your opponent's backhand is significantly weaker than his forehand, you would factor that into your serving strategy. You might decide to go against the percentages and serve consistently to the player's weak backhand or, you could serve down the middle more often, and wait for a big point to serve to their weaker side.

At the 4.0 level and above serving strategy and serving patterns become extremely important. If you give your opponent the same serve, to the same spot, time after time, it won't be long before they get grooved and have their rackets back before you even toss the ball.

Mix up the placement, spin and pace of your serves. This will keep them guessing and often force a weak return which you or your partner can move forward and volley offensively.

Serve & Sprint

With a high percentage of first serves in your favor your next task is to move forward, join your partner at the net and gain control of the point. This is the major advantage in serving: your team has a head start in that all-important race to control the net.

When serving and volleying, keep in mind that a hard, flat serve may do you more harm than good. The faster your serves moves, the faster it will come back to you. This means that you'll have less time to advance to, and get settled at, the net. Throw in the occasional flat serve but, for the most part, stick with spin serves as they'll allow you more time to advance to the net.

After you've completed your serve and are on your way to the net, you'll have time for approximately 3-4 running steps. At that point your serve will have crossed the net, bounced, and your opponent is getting ready to hit their return. This is the time to execute your split-step, see where the return is coming, and then move to get it. Many players make the mistake of taking their split-step and then waiting for the volley to come to them. Go and get it! Strive to hit your first volley from inside the service line.

Seldom will your first volley be the shot that you will win the point with. Yes, if your opponent pops up a short, high return, you may be able to move in and put the ball away by volleying at the feet of the receiver's partner, but don't plan on it.

The vast majority of the time, the best play is to simply return the volley back deep to the player who returned the serve. You can then settle in at the net with your partner and begin your movement and anticipation strategies.

Words From the Wise

Coaching legend Nick Bollettieri says, "Never try for a winner on your first volley. Your objective should be accurate placement." Bollettieri who's coached nine world #1 players, says that "The object of the first volley is to set up a second, easier volley. Dare your opponents to pass you. If you hit a solid first volley, you'll succeed more often than not."

Players often ask me if they should come in behind their second serve. It depends. If the serve resembles a slow moving balloon to come in would be tennis suicide. Stay back and hope to get in on a subsequent shot.

Ultimately though, your goal should be to serve and volley on both serves. To do so means that you must develop strong first and second serves, which will allow you to move in without the threat of having your head taken off.

If you're not confident enough with your serve to come in, you're basically putting up for grabs two or three games a set that should be heavily weighted in your favor. If your partner is in the same boat, serve-wise, then your team is really going to struggle.

Moral: develop a consistent first and second serve where you can vary the direction, spin and pace. This will allow you to confidently serve and volley and control the majority of points during your service game.

Possessing a strong serve that allows you to effectively serve and volley gives your team a huge advantage in a high level doubles match. However, it does take two to tango and in the next chapter, I'll show you how, by working with your partner, you'll be a good bet to win your service games every time!

7

Control the Game without Touching the Ball

What to do while your partner serves

Many players seem to view their partner's service games as a break, time off the job. They frequently stand at the net and watch their partner play. Sure, they'll hit the ball if it happens to come to them but, if their team loses the game they think, "Hey, it wasn't my fault. I won my service game."

Sorry, but when your partner is serving, you are as much responsible for the outcome of the game as he is. In fact, with the right approach, you can control the game without ever touching the ball.

Where to Stand

Mary and Ann are two top USTA doubles players. As you can see below, when Mary lines up to serve, Ann positions herself roughly halfway between the service line and the net, in the middle of the service box.

Then, depending upon where Mary serves, Ann will adjust her position accordingly. If she serves out wide (1), Ann will follow the ball out wide. If the serve goes down the middle (2), she'll move a step towards the center and look to poach. Of course, this is all predetermined before the point begins.

As the match goes on and you get a feel for your opponent's skills and tendencies, you'll continue to make adjustments. Doubles at its best is a game where both teams are constantly analyzing and adjusting to each other's strengths, weaknesses and tendencies. Pay attention! If you notice that the receiver never returns down the line, you can move a bit more towards the center. If he never lobs, move in a few feet.

Stay away from these two common errors:

1. **Lining up too close to the sideline.** The thought here is to protect the alley but this approach usually does more harm than good. First, it shows the receiver a big space down the center of the court which will undoubtedly help them relax on their return. Plus, it makes it virtually impossible for you to poach. If your partner serves wide, then shift over towards the alley. If your opponent constantly tries to go down your alley, then line up closer to the sideline for a point or two and then move right back to the center of the service box. Remember, constantly adjust.

2. **Lining up too close to the net:** If your opponent never lobs, this might be a good strategy but a smart player will notice that you're too close to the net and immediately start going over your head. This will allow the other team to advance and take control of the net - the last thing your team wants.

Ultimate Chaos

As your partner prepares to serve, bounce up and down and move side to side. Look hungry! The next time you see the Bryan brothers play, notice their bodies before each point begins. They look as if they're ready to jump out of their shoes. This energy sends a message to their opponents: we're coming to get you! Your goal is to get the receiver thinking more about you than he is about returning the serve.

When your partner is serving, your job is to create chaos among your opponents. Get in the receiver's face: move around, poach and fake. Take the attitude that every ball they hit is yours.

Words From the Wise

USPTA pro and former touring professional, Rayni Fox-Borinsky has her ladies play Decade Tennis. "I tell them that for every decade they play, they should stand another foot or two away from the net when their partner serves!

Players should take into account how well they can cover the lob over their head because they're useless if their opponents know that a mediocre lob will be effective in getting them off balance and scampering to regroup."

The key to playing this position effectively is to anticipate whether the return of serve is going to be a lob or a drive. Watch the receiver's body and racket face. If they're moving forward and their racket is at the same height of the ball, they're probably going to drive their return. Immediately take two steps forward and look to move diagonally to pick off the shot.

If you notice that your opponent is off balance, leaning back and their racket drops below the height of the ball and the face opens up, it's going to be a lob. Quickly take three steps back.

Once you get a feel for whether the return is going to be a lob or drive, your next thought is "This shot is mine." Don't be surprised when the ball comes to you. Be surprised when you can't hit it.

Your top priority is to make the receiving team aware, no, make that AFRAID, of you. This fear will force them into attempting low percentage returns, which will result in many, many errors.

The Slam Dunk

Nothing feels better on the doubles court than anticipating an opponent's return, moving across the net, and drilling a volley right between the legs of their helpless partner.

When your team executes a successful poach to end the point, you're making a statement. You're saying: "We're here to play and we're going to be in your face for the entire match!"

Poaching is a fabulous way to take opposing teams out of their rhythm yet, for many players, it's a scary proposition. I can't tell you how often I watch recreational doubles where two players are standing on the baseline exchanging ground strokes while their respective partners remain virtually motionless at the net. The only part of their bodies that moves are their heads, as they watch the ball go back and forth.

This is not doubles! It's singles with two statues. High level doubles is a game of quick movements, fast exchanges and lots of poaching! Professional doubles teams win thousands of points each year poaching. Your team can as well.

When you and your partner commit to poaching, your team immediately becomes stronger in two ways. First, you'll gain the ability to end points in a quick and intimidating manner. Second and, in my opinion, most important, when you're active at the net, you'll forever keep your opponents off-balance.

Poaching falls into two categories. The first is what I like to call the "there it is poach." This is when you see a weak return and then cross in front of your partner to go after it. Actually, I don't really consider this poaching, it's common sense! If you're standing at the net and your opponent hits a feeble, floating return, you're supposed to go after it. That's your job!

True poaching, in my opinion, falls under the "here I go" category. This means that you've decided to make a move before your opponent actually strikes their shot. It's risky, exciting, and, when executed correctly, immediately takes the wind out of your opponent's sails.

When to Poach

Though the opportunity to poach can arise at any moment, the easiest way to get started is when your team is serving because you and your partner can set it up before the point begins. This is what's going on when you see the pros using hand signals. They're setting up a play. They decide where the serve is going and whether the net player is going to poach, fake or stay.

Much like a catcher calling pitches in baseball, you'll signal to your serving partner before each point. You can tell him where you want the serve to be hit and what you're going to do after.

Signals, which should be given behind your back with your non-racket hand, can be simple such as:

Open hand: I'm poaching

Closed hand: I'm faking a poach

Or, they can become more detailed such as:

Open hand, one finger pointing: Serve to the "T". I'm poaching.

Open hand, two finders pointing: Serve into the body. I'm poaching. Closed hand, thumb up: Serve out wide. I'll fake a poach.

If the server, for some reason, doesn't like the signal, he can verbally shake you off by saying "No" and then you'll give him another.

Hand signals are a great way to plan a point but your team must stay sharp as far as remembering first, what the signals mean and then making sure to consistently use them.

It doesn't have to be every point but just be sure to use them enough to keep your opponents guessing. I once saw a doubles team only use hand signals when they planned to serve down the middle and have the net player poach. It didn't take the receiving team long to figure this out and drill a return down the poacher's alley, every time.

I actually prefer to have my players communicate verbally. After each point, most teams have a brief meeting. The conversation is usually something simple such as "nice shot or good try." Occasionally it gets nasty as one partner might snarl to the other, "how could you miss that, or that ball was mine."

Words From the Wise

Master Professional, Ken Dehart says that "Many players will only tell their partner where their first serve is going", says Ken. "Then, if they miss, their partner has no idea what to expect on the second serve.

Ken suggests the following system when serving: "The server should tell the net player "I am going to serve C – B. This means, first serve up the center and second serve into the body. They may also use A - C, first serve toward the alley and second serve up the center. Using A, B and C for targets on the first and second serves will make it easy to communicate an easy plan of action so the serving team is on the same page.

Telling your partner where you plan to direct both serves keeps the server focused when the first serve has failed and the net player has a better idea on how to plan their action at the net.

Personalities aside, the point is that, during these brief meetings you can also set up your play for the next point. For example: "serve down the middle and I'm going to go" or "serve out wide and I'll fake." That's it. It takes two seconds, doesn't disrupt the flow of play and both you and your partner are clear as to what's going to happen.

Now the Fun Begins

You've set up the play: your partner is going to serve towards the "T" and you're going to move across the court and nail the volley. Now comes the tricky part. The key to successful poaching lies in the timing. If you move too soon your opponent will have time to adapt and if you move too late, you won't be able to catch up to their ball.

As your opponent moves towards their shot and you've made the decision to poach, begin moving closer to the net. Keep your eyes glued to his racket head. When you see that he's begun his forward swing into the ball, you know he's committed to his shot. Now is the time to make your move!

Push off your outside leg and, moving diagonally towards the net, sprint across the court. By moving at a forward angle, you'll get closer to the net and also cut off your opponent's shot sooner, giving them less time to react.

Where Do I Hit My Volley?

One of the risks in poaching is that, since you are moving before your opponent strikes the ball, you don't know what type of shot you're going to have to play. If all goes as planned, you've got a nice fat ball to volley.

Where are you going to hit it? You're going to drill it right at the feet of the opposing net player as shown below. She's closer to you and, as a result, has less time to react.

I can't tell you how often I see club players execute a perfectly timed poach only to then volley the ball back to the baseline player. That player then, with a huge smile on his face, drives a winner right back down the poachers vacated side of the court. This is one of those times when the between point meetings might elicit a nasty remark.

If you've poached and are facing a strong low shot, have no fear, you still have a play. As the ball is low, you'll have to volley "up" so you want to be sure to keep it away from the opposing net player. To do so, try a soft, angled, drop volley, crosscourt. This is not an easy shot to execute so if you don't feel you can control the ball, volley back to the baseline player. Yes, your side of the court is still wide open but hopefully your partner has begun moving to cover it—as he should.

What Next?

Once you've moved across the court and picked off your opponent's shot, you then have to make a quick strategic decision: where do you move next? If you've made contact with the ball on your partner's side of the court, keep going. If you've struck the ball on your side of the court, jump back.

If the pace is too quick and you don't know what to do, just do something! Frequently I'll see players, after they've picked off a volley, lose sight of where they are in the court and freeze in the middle. If this happens, just pick a side and quickly move there. Your partner can then react accordingly.

Other Poaching Possibilities

Aside from the return of serve, here are two other scenarios to look to poach.

1. **When your opponent is hitting their inside groundstroke**. By "inside" I mean a ball towards the center of their court. When they're hitting from the center, they'll be swinging away from their body, which for most players will produce a weaker shot.

Plus, from the center of the court, the chances of an opponent being able to create a sharp angle, back into your alley, are slim. You can be relatively certain that they'll be hitting back to your partner so your poaching antenna should go up.

2. **When your partner is returning serve against a serve and volley player**. When facing a serve and volley player, the receiver's goal is to return the serve down low at his feet. When faced with this difficult volley, the odds are that the opponent will hit the percentage shot, which is back to the receiver.

As the receiver's partner, look for those low returns. When you spot one, take two quick steps forward and then, just before contact, move diagonally across the net, pick off the volley and end the point with a strong volley of your own.

A quick aside: always beware of poaching when your partner hits their shot wide. Wide shots are hit on an angle and angles are often returned with angles. Your opponent's return will often be traveling at an angle that will be too difficult for you to reach. Plus, when pulled wide, they also have a straight shot down the line so you must move to cover your alley.

If Disaster Strikes

You've picked your ball to poach, made a good move, and the worst possible scenario occurs: your opponent drives the ball behind you, into your alley for a winner. Now what do you do?

You feel embarrassed, apologize to your partner and never poach again, right? Wrong! You say "nice shot," move onto the next point - and immediately look to poach again.

To be an effective force at the net you must have a thick skin. I tell my players that if they attempt to poach ten times during the course of a set they'll probably be a hero 4-6 times and look like an idiot the rest. "So what's the point," they frequently ask.

The point is that, by being active at the net, you'll create an atmosphere of uncertainty with

Words From the Wise

Michigan teaching pro Mike Woody is famous for telling his students that "the worst doubles players never gets burned down the alley. In fact, if you never get burned down the alley you might want to reconsider your doubles prowess.

The "best" doubles players in the world occasionally get passed down the alley because they are big picture thinkers and are looking to cover the middle and intercept shots."

Mike suggests the following exercise to help your team gauge its level of aggressiveness.

"During your next match keep count of shots made and missed down the alley by your opponent. For every missed shot your opponent makes in an attempt to hit down your alley —give yourself a point, for every winner your opponent makes down the alley take away a point. After six games, check the score.

If you have positive points, then continue to focus on covering the middle and being very active at the net. Keep teasing your opponent to go up the line, it's paying off. If you are in the negatives you might conclude that you are giving your opponent too much room or you might want to do more fake poaching and stay home."

your opponents. If you play the net like a statue, they'll have no fear and be much more relaxed and able to swing away. If you're opponents never hit down your alley, it's a clear signal that you're not being aggressive enough.

However if you're up on your toes, poaching, faking and moving as they prepare to return, you'll keep them off balance. By planting the seed in your opponent's mind that you might poach, you'll force them into many weak shots and errors. This is the, not so apparent, benefit of poaching.

Always remember not to gauge your poaching success by the number of times you hit a winning volley or how often you lose the point. Until you get to a very high level, and develop superior poaching skills, those two things may very well balance out.

The next time you and your partner take the court, commit to trying 1-2 poaches each game. Be patient and, as your poaching skill improves, you'll see that the true benefit of being active at the net is the pressure you'll put on your opponents each and every time they take their racket back.

Here's a great drill to sharpen your poaching skills:

You'll need two of your tennis buddies: one to serve and one to return serve.

Have the server practice serving to the T, which is the most important serve to have in doubles. The receiver practices his inside out return and you practice timing your poach. After 10 serves, rotate positions. Once each player has practiced from all three spots, go around again only this time the person receiving serve has the option of trying to hit down the net player's alley.

More Strategies to Ensure Victory

Football, baseball and basketball teams all have different formations and plays. Your team should as well. Here are two other formations that your team can use when serving that will keep your opponents guessing.

The Australian Formation

First used by the great Australian doubles teams, this clever formation has won Mary and Ann many matches. In this setup shown below, Mary positions herself on the same half of the court, in front of, Ann.

After serving, Ann will then move diagonally forward to join Mary at the net. This is a great strategy against players who have strong cross-court returns of serve. By positioning Mary on the same side as Ann, they're saying to the receiver that "you can't hit your great cross-court return, unless you want to hit it right to Mary who's in a great position to hit an offensive volley.

Most players are grooved to return serve cross-court a majority of the time. The Australian formation takes them out of their comfort zone and forces them to hit down the line. Plus, from this formation, Mary can fake and poach which will further disrupt the receiver.

Mary says, "We once played a doubles match against a player who had a fabulous cross-court return from the ad side. It didn't matter where we served or how active we were at the net. She consistently killed us cross-court. We moved to the Australian formation and the poor girl didn't get another return of serve back in play the entire match.

The "I" Formation

This is another variation designed to get your opponents scratching their head. This one's a bit more advanced ...and risky. Here, Mary lines up in the center of the court, one foot on either side of the center service line.

As Ann prepares to serve, Mary crouches down as low as she can. After the serve crosses the net, she'll quickly move to one side while Ann moves forward to the other. Again, this was predetermined prior to the point either verbally or via a hand signal. This keeps Mary and Ann's opponents off balance and can work for you too.

Use these formations as often or as little as you like. Mix it up between the standard setup, the Australian, the "I" and remember to run your plays. Be active, fake and poach. If you find your team is behind, remind yourselves that momentum can change at the drop of a hat. Throw in some different formations to upset your opponent's rhythm.

Remember, a good serving team has three advantages working for them: a strong serve which will keep the receiver off-balance, an aggressive server who follows his delivery to the net, and finally, an active net player who is constantly moving, faking and poaching.

That's three "pressures" that the receiving team must deal with and that is exactly why, in high-level tennis, service breaks are a rare occurrence.

8

React & Attack: Winning Service Returns

How to turn the tables on the serving team

Tennis experts tell us that the serving team in a doubles match has a huge advantage over their opponents. They hit the first shot of the point and, as a result, have a head start in winning that all-important race to the net.

With the combination of a strong player, who is able to mix up his serves, and an active partner at the net, the serving team is often able to force weak returns or errors. Once those weak returns are hit, the team is able to move forward, end the point with a strong volley or, at the very least, take control of the point by having both players at the net.

Though the team holding the balls at the start of the point may appear to have an initial advantage, the good news is that, with good technique and smart tactics, you can minimize their head start and ultimately take control of the point.

Technique

Once you reach the 4.0 level and above you'll see some big serves. Players at the upper levels of the game can frequently serve at speeds 85 m.p.h. and higher. At this pace, you'll have a little over half a second to figure out where the serve is going, if and how it's spinning, and then execute a quality return. That's not a lot of time but with proper positioning before the serve, an active ready position and a plan, you can make your return of serve a weapon.

How Much Time Do I have?

Below are the approximate reaction times you'll have when facing serves at different speeds.

Speed of serve (mph)	Reaction time (seconds)
90	.59
80	.66
70	.76
60	.88
50	1.06

Develop a Return of Serve Ritual

As with the serve, a return of serve ritual will help you relax, focus and prepare to hit your best return. Again, a ritual is a very personal thing. Here's what I do before every point:

1. Walk back with my eyes focused on my strings and touch the back fence with my racket.

2. Move back towards the court, eyes still focused on strings.

3. Step into position, left foot first then right. Head looking down at the court.

4. Shift weight from my left foot to my right three times, head still down.

5. Look up signaling that I'm ready.

This simple routine helps me clear my head and allows me to mentally prepare for the next point.

Where to Stand

As you're preparing to receive serve, you need to ask yourself two questions:

1. How close in can I get?

2. How far over should I be?

Initially, line up as close to (or inside of) the baseline as possible. This will allow you to quickly return the ball before the server is able to move into a strong net position. If you're facing a big serve, you can back up accordingly.

In terms of how far over you should be, take your cues from the server. An experienced server will vary his or her positions along the baseline. You should as well. If the server moves more towards the center of their court, move towards yours. If he moves out wide, slide over to cut off the probable angle.

As the match progresses, take note of the server's strengths and tendencies and adjust your position (up or back, and left or right) accordingly. Many players serve to the same spot every single time while others will give you a clue as to where they're serving by how they stand or where they toss the ball. For example, if the toss is to the left of the server's body, move to your left. If he tosses the ball wide to his right side, move to your right.

Andre Agassi, who possessed arguably the greatest return of serve in the history of the game revealed a secret that he held each time he played German legend Boris Becker. It seems Becker had a habit of sticking his tongue out to the side of his mouth before he served. Andre noticed that if Becker's tongue went to the right, so did his serve and vice versa. Imagine knowing where your opponent was going to serve before he even tossed up the ball? What an advantage!

As you wait for the serve, be up on your toes and have a general idea of what you want to do with your return based on the server's style of play and your ultimate goal of getting to the net. If you're facing a serve and volley opponent, focus on returning the ball down low at their feet and then moving in. If you're opponent serves and stays back, plan on aiming 2-3 feet above the net, return the ball crosscourt and deep and then get to the net as soon as possible.

Just before the serve is struck, take a strong split step and see the ball come off your opponent's strings. Once you've determined which direction the serve is coming, immediately turn your shoulders and pivot your feet towards the oncoming ball.

This quick shoulder turn will begin your racket preparation. At this point, sneak a glance at the server to see if he's coming in or staying back. Then, you can choose how you're going to hit your return from these options:

Words From the Wise

To sharpen your reflexes when returning serve, Master Professional Jimmy Pitkanen suggests that, "when practicing your return, ask the server to move up to just behind the service line. With less distance between you and the server, you'll be forced to improve your reaction time to get the ball back."

1. **Block it:** This works best against a big serve. Shorten your backswing and keep your stroke very compact. Focus on pointing your strings to where you want the ball to go and imagine a volley with a follow-through. Plan for a two shot combination: punch the ball down low, forcing the oncoming server to volley up. You or your partner can then move forward and pick off the weak volley.

A variation of this would be the "chip & charge return." With this strategy, you hit a soft slice to the oncoming server's feet and then sprint forward, trying to beat the server to the net. Use a shorter and slightly higher (about ear level, backswing). Then, while moving into the shot, swing down along the backside of the ball, putting backspin on your shot. The goal is to make the ball bounce in front of the oncoming server. Because of the spin, when the ball bounces, it will stay very low and force the player to hit up to you and your partner. It's a great play but requires a lot of touch, particularly against a strong serve. Try it when your opponent comes in on their second serve.

2. **Drive it:** As the game continues to evolve and rackets become lighter and athletes faster, more and more players are able to drive the ball on their return, even off of a strong serve. If your opponent has a serve that you feel you can get around on and execute a full groundstroke, go for it. However, don't be reckless.

Remember, your primary goal with the return of serve is to **return the serve**. Do not attempt to tee off and go for an outright winner. Very rarely will you be able to end the point with your return of serve. You can though, take away much of the server's advantage with a strong topspin drive.

Prepare as you would for any other return. The difference being, when you execute your shoulder turn, you'll bring the racket back a bit further than you would for the block return. This will enable you to generate more racket head speed and hit a stronger ball.

Words From the Wise

When driving the ball, tennis legend Tony Trabert suggests thinking of your strokes in terms of an airplane versus a helicopter. Trabert says, "When you watch an airplane take off what does it do? It travels down the runway, gathering speed until it begins a gradual angled ascent. A helicopter takes off vertically or straight up."

"When you are hitting forehands or backhands, pretend that your racket is an airplane, not a helicopter. As you begin your swing, the racket should travel down the runway, picking up speed as it goes."

If, as expected, the server is coming in, try to drive the ball at his feet and force a weak return. You can then move forward into the net. If he stays back, aim higher over the net, roll the ball deep and join your partner at the net.

3.   **Lob it**: This one's my favorite because, if executed well, it can immediately take away the serving team's advantage and put your team in the driver's seat. You can hit it with the same short backswing that you use for your block or chip return, simply open the racket face on contact and push the ball over the server's partner's head. You can then join your partner at the net and gain the advantage.

Tactics

"The most important thing to remember when returning serve from a tactical standpoint," says Tom Gullikson, "is to get the ball back in play. Don't give your opponents any roses."

R (return) O (of) S (serve) E (errors)

Gully's right. Whether you're receiving serve in a 3.0 league, center court at Wimbledon or somewhere in between, your first goal is to get the ball back in play and make your opponents hit their next shot. However, as your team begins to compete against stronger players, you'll need to take your tactics to the next level.

Just as the serving team sets up a play before the point begins, the receiving team can as well. Before the point begins, let your partner know where you're going to hit your return: crosscourt, down the alley, right at the net man or lob. This helps your team in two important ways:

1.   Once the serve is hit, your partner can position himself accordingly. For example, if he knows that you'll be returning at the net man, he can quickly move towards the center of the court and if the volley is high, he can then move in and pounce on the weak return.

2. By deciding where you're going to hit your return beforehand you'll take away that brief moment of indecision and be able to focus on hitting a solid ball towards your target.

When you are receiving serve keep these tactical goals in mind:

· Get the ball back in play.

· Keep your return away from the server's active partner.

· If the server follows his shot to the net, aim down at his feet. Force him to volley "up" at which point you, or your partner, can move in to aggressively volley the high return.

· If the server stays back, return your shot deep and crosscourt and move to the net.

Take the Server's Partner Out of the Point

As I mentioned earlier, when receiving serve, your team will undoubtedly have to deal with an aggressive net player, so you must come up with a way to keep that player under control. This can be done by hitting the occasional shot down the alley.

I always try to go down the net player's alley early in a match. Even if he or she volleys the ball away, it's worth the loss of an early point because I've planted the seed that lets the net player know that I might go there, and this will make the net player a bit more hesitant to poach. We'll look at the strategy of hitting down the alley in the next chapter.

Another option would be to drive your return right at the opposing net man. Again, this will keep him on his toes and a little less eager to poach. Finally you can lob over his head. By keeping the net player guessing, he'll always have that moment of indecision and, as a result, be much less effective.

Develop a Return of Serve Mantra

Finally, when your team is retuning serve, repeat the words "react" and "attack" to each other throughout the game. This means simply that on your opponent's first (stronger) serve you focus on reacting as quickly as possible and hitting a low return away from the net player.

If the first serve is missed, think attack! Move up a couple of steps and get ready to jump on the second (usually weaker) serve. Drive the return back cross-court and move up to the net. If your opponent follows his second serve in, aim low, force him to pop the ball up, and then make him pay.

Though the serving team may hold an early advantage, by incorporating these techniques and tactics you can turn your return games into offensive opportunities for your team.

9

Stay Away From Dark Alleys

When and when not to hit down the alley

For many players, the doubles alley holds a mysterious fascination. Though visually it's a small target, a big shot between the lines can be as tempting as that midnight bowl of ice cream.

As I work with doubles players round the country I notice that many want to know when, and when not, to attempt a shot down their opponent's alley. Point after point, players try to fire the ball past their opponent, only to be frustrated by their own errors or easily put away volleys by an alert net player.

Usually it's the big hitters who suffer from alley obsession. These are players whose top priority is to burn the cover off the ball as they rip a shot past their helpless opponent. In their minds, the person who hits the ball the hardest is the better player, regardless of where the ball lands or what the scoreboard says at the end of the match. For these macho men and women, "percentage" is a dirty word yet the fact is that the down the alley shot is a low percentage play.

Ten-time Grand Slam doubles champion Anne Smith agrees. "Hitting down the line to the alley either on the return of serve or during the point is one of the lowest percentage shots in doubles." This is true for a variety of reasons. To begin with, the alley is an extremely small area of the court (just 54 inches wide), plus the net is six inches higher at the corners.

Also, to place a shot ball down your opponent's alley, you'll often have to change the direction of the oncoming ball, which is a challenging task. Even if you do hit the shot well, you've given your opponent two easy options to beat you: they can volley the ball away down the middle or drill it at your partner.

Finally, by hitting to the outside of the court, you're presenting your opponent with many angles to play with their return. "When all is said and done," says Smith, author of the book Grand Slam: Coach your Mind to Win in Sports, Business and Life, "this strategy does not give you the best opportunity to win the point."

Does this mean that you should never venture down your opponent's alley: of course not. If used at the appropriate time, the shot can be a tremendous weapon and have a dramatic impact on your matches. When then is that "right" time?

In doubles there are three scenarios in which you would try to hit the ball down your opponent's alley:

1. **If they leave the alley open**—Let's say your opponent has pulled you out wide with a heavy slice serve. As you move to the ball, you sneak a quick glance and notice that the opposing net player hasn't shifted (as he should) to cover his alley. Knowing that the straight, down the line shot is the fastest way to get the ball past your opponent, a hard drive down the alley can most definitely win you the point and deflate your opponent at the same time.

2. **Your opponent volleys poorly or isn't mentally alert**—This one's a no-brainer. If the opposing net player appears afraid of the net, doesn't volley well or looks unfocused, simply keep hitting to

their alley (or right at them) until they miss enough shots to win you the match.

3. **Your opponent is actively poaching**—The server's partner is driving you crazy each time you prepare to strike the ball (as he or she should). He's moving, faking, poaching, and basically has you so nervous you can barely take your racket back. Then, a hard drive down the alley can be a useful tactic. By hitting the occasional shot down this player's alley or again right at them, you're telling him that you can, and will hit there. This will undoubtedly force him to be less bold and aggressive.

While these are all excellent situations to drive the ball down your opponent's alley, you must keep in mind that, at the 4.0 level and above, the first two of those three scenarios largely disappear.

At the higher levels of the game, experienced players understand court positioning and will move as they should. This means that if your opponent hits a shot that pulls you out wide, his net-playing partner, ninety-nine percent of the time, will shift to cover his alley.

As you prepare to hit, take a quick look and if the player hasn't shifted, go for it. However, if he has moved as he should, don't force it. If you do, your opponent will most likely have a huge smile on his face as he easily ends the point with a volley down the center of the court, between you and your partner.

Alley is covered. Stay away.   **Alley is open. Go for it!**

Strong players usually like the net, are alert, and volley well. This means that if you hit down their alley they will, again, be quite willing and able to end the point with a put away volley. That leaves you with only one true scenario in which you should be attempting to drive the ball down your opponent's alley: if he or she is actively poaching.

10

Hero or Target - The Receiver's Partner

How to thrive in this awkward position

When your partner's returning serve, you're squarely in the hot seat. If he does his job and hits an effective return, you can move forward, pick off your opponents shots and be a hero. If he hits a return that your opponents can attack you'll be a target with your only goal being self-preservation.

A feast or famine position to say the least, however, with the right strategy you can turn this hot spot into an advantage for your team.

Where to stand

From a positioning standpoint, you have three choices at the start of each point:

1. Begin the point on the service line

2. Begin the point 1-2 feet in front of the service line

3. Begin the point at the baseline

If you're not familiar with your opponents, begin the match on the service line. As the match progresses and you develop a feel for the opposing team, as well as how your partner is returning serve, you can make adjustments.

When facing an opponent with a weak serve, a net player who never poaches or if your teammate is having a great day returning, move a foot or two in front of the service line. This will put pressure on your opponents because now, you're in a position to move forward after the return and do some real damage.

On those days when your partner is struggling with his service return, you may very well want to move back to the baseline on your opponent's first serve. You see this frequently at the professional level where players are often facing serves well over 100 m.p.h.

Yes, you're conceding the race to the net but you'll give your team a better chance of staying in the point after a weak service return. Though having both players positioned at the baseline is a defensive strategy, it can actually be quite effective against an aggressive team. I'll explain how in chapter 13.

If the first serve is missed, you can then move back up to the service line. Presumably your partner will hit a strong return off of the second serve and you can then begin to think offensively.

Finally, at the 4.0 level and above, you'll most likely be facing a strong serve and volley player as well as his active partner at the net. As your partner prepares to return serve, stand at an angle so that you're facing the server's partner. He's the immediate threat to your team. By standing at this angle, you'll be able to watch and react to his movements much quicker.

Make a Quick Assessment

Once you hear your partner strike their return, you need to determine as quickly as possible what type of return he's hit and assess the situation. Contrary to popular opinion, this is NOT done by turning and watching your partner hit the ball.

When you turn your head to look at your partner, as in the diagram, you lose sight of what the serving team is doing and this can be physically dangerous. If the opposing net player decides to poach, by the time you get your head turned back around, the next thing you may see are stars after receiving a "fuzz sandwich" compliments of the poacher's volley.

Focus your attention on the player serving. Then, as soon as he strikes the ball, shift your gaze to his partner. Look in his eyes and read his body language and you'll have all the information you'll need.

Not looking back to watch your partner hit the ball will take some getting used to. We've all been told since we began playing to always keep our eyes on the ball but, the fact is there are certain instances when watching a particular player will give you a better clue as to what's coming than watching the ball.

You'll be surprised by how this little bit of extra time gained by watching the server's partner, instead of your own, will allow you to prepare and hopefully, return a few more balls that in the past you've only been able to protect yourself from.

When your partner returns serve, there are basically five scenarios:

1. **A weak return that the server or his partner is going to attack.**

   Pay attention to the net player's eyes and body language. If you see them widen and he quickly starts moving across the court, he's poaching. Get your hands up, take a strong split step and do the best you can to react to the hard volley which will soon be upon you.

Words From the Wise

To break the habit of looking back at your partner as he hits the ball, USPTA Pro Paula Scheb suggests viewing your opponents as "two mean dogs that live on your street. One is in the house at the end of the block and the other is in the house across the street. Which dog do you pay attention to first? The one next door."

"Always keep your eyes on the dog that's most likely to bite you - the opposing net player."

If the ball moves past him high, immediately shift your eyes toward the server. If he's moving forward and foaming at the mouth, again prepare to react quickly because he's probably going to drive his shot right at you.

2. **A strong, low return to the net rushing server**

   When the server's partner's body language remains calm, and the ball moves low past him, it's your turn to get excited. When the server is moving forward, the low return will force him to volley up. Look to poach. From this difficult position, the odds of him volleying down your alley are slim. To do so he must dig the ball up off the court, change it's direction and then hit the ball over the highest part of the net.

   All of these combined tell you that he's probably going to volley back to your partner. Just before he makes contact, shoot across the court on a diagonal, pick off his volley and end the point with an aggressive shot down the middle.

Though this is not a situation where players generally think to poach, with a strong return of serve and quick reaction, it can be a devastating play. Even if you don't reach the volley you've planted the seed in your opponent's mind that you might poach.

Words From the Wise

As you prepare to volley, USPTA Master Professional Mike O'Connell suggests imagining yourself as a boxer in the ring. "Think of how boxers hold their hands during a fight. They keep them in front of their faces not only for protection, but also so they can strike quickly. If you keep your racket up and in front of your body for volleys, you'll be more prepared and make better contact. "

3. A deep return to the server who's stayed back

If your partner has hit a deep cross-court return, and the server has not followed his serve to the net, you then shift into attack mode. Follow the ball forward and look to be aggressive.

4. A return at the opposing net player

When your partner returns the serve low toward the opposing net player, immediately start moving diagonally towards him. Because the ball is low, he may very well pop his shot up. When that happens, you'll be there to pick it off. Plus, if he feels you coming at him, it will make an awkward shot even more difficult.

If the return of serve is high, and you see your opponent move forward, he's probably going to hit an aggressive volley between you and your partner. Quickly move to the center and try to hit a reflex volley.

When you see the net player preparing to hit an overhead, backpedal and then, just before the ball is struck, take a strong split step and balance yourself. Many players feel that they need to get back as far as they can to reply to an oncoming overhead. As a result, they're often caught still backing up as the ball is struck. Now, they're totally off-balance and faced with a rocket coming right at them. You're much better off being a bit closer to the net but balanced and stable. From this position you'll best be able to react to the shot and, if necessary, protect yourself.

With a *really* weak return that makes you feel physically threatened, abandon ship. Take a crossover step, turn your back and move towards your doubles alley. Give him the big hole down the center. Don't be a hero, concede the point and live to fight the next point.

5. A lob

If your partner lobs his return of serve over the opposing net player, and both players are scrambling back to chase the ball, be careful. You'll see your opponents in trouble and your instincts will undoubtedly tell you and your partner to charge the net. Not so fast!

Strong players, when they're on the defensive, know that their best option is to hit a high defensive lob. If you and your partner are both charging the net, you might get caught.

Instead, when you see your opponents scrambling back for a lob, both you and your partner should position yourselves on or around the service line. Then, when the likely lob comes, you're ready for it. If it's a weak shot, you can always move forward to play the ball. Yes, from the service line position you're vulnerable to a low drive but, if both opponents are struggling to get to the ball, that shot is unlikely.

As the receiver's partner you are firmly planted on the hot seat. However by learning to keep your eyes forward, assess, and react properly, you can not only survive this treacherous position, but even turn the heat onto your opponents.

I'm often asked if it's the receiver's partner's job to call the serve in or out. I say "generally, no."You have enough to worry about trying to react to your partner's shot. Once the serve is hit, your focus should immediately shift to the opposing net player. If your opponent has a huge serve and your partner simply can't concentrate on calling the serve and trying to hit it back, then call the line. Just be sure to get your eyes back on the server's partner ASAP!

11

Three Shots and You Win

A great shot in singles can be a poor shot for doubles

"Hit 'em where they ain't." These are the words that most players heard when they first began to study tennis strategy. What this famous phrase means is that your goal is to hit your shots to the open space so that your opponent won't be able to touch the ball and you'll win the point. While this is certainly sound advice when you're playing singles, for those who play doubles on a regular basis, it's a poor percentage play.

As the ball travels back and forth across the net, an experienced doubles team will consistently shift from side to side (following the ball) and position themselves so that the only "open" space on the court is the spot that's most difficult for your team to hit. For example:

Mac and Betsy are playing mixed doubles and their opponents have taken the net. Mac, playing the ad court, has been pulled out wide. As he moves to hit his backhand, his experienced opponents immediately shift in the same direction. Here's what Mac's looking at as he prepares to hit his shot.

As you can see from the diagram, the only "open" space for Mac to hit is that small area of the court to his far right marked by the "X". To hit it, so that his opponent's can't reach it, Mac will have to execute, on the run and under pressure, a sharply angled low shot to approximately a 2-3 foot space.

Can he do it? Sure, if his name's Bob or Mike Bryan. For Mac, and the rest of us, that shot has about a 10-15 percent chance of being successful. The rest of the time, we'll either hit the ball wide, or into the net, giving our opponents a huge psychological advantage.

Strong doubles teams constantly shift side to side and up and back so that the only "open" spaces they leave are the ones that are the most difficult to hit. They tease their opponents into going for the low percentage play and feast on their errors.

Don't fall into their trap. Be like Mac and stay away from the "hit 'em where they ain't" approach. Let the other team go for the clean winners. They'll hit a few but over the course of a long match they'll miss far more than they'll make. They can have their clean winners while you and your partner win the match.

Each time you and your partner take the court, commit to beating your opponents by hitting to three places: down the middle, at their feet or over their heads.

Down the Middle

This is a smart shot for several reasons:

1. A shot hit down the middle of the court crosses the net at the center, the lowest part.

2. Your opponents will always feel a sense of confusion over who should take the shot.

3. By hitting down the middle you offer your opponents no angles with which to respond. When you hit to the outsides of the court, your opponents have many angles at their disposal. When you play down the center, they must create their own angle, which is not easy to do.

4. When you hit down the center, if you don't hit the ball well, you'll probably still keep it in play. Aiming for the outsides of the court, if you miss your target, you'll most likely hit the ball out of the court.

Tennis legend, Vic Braden, says that "I've long been fascinated by the intermediates who say 'Watch your alley,' while the pros are always talking about protecting the middle. Intermediates are so afraid of their opponents hitting down the line that one of them plays wide to the left and the other wide to the right. Unfortunately, they're one man short."

"You could drive a truck between them. They're so intent on guarding their alleys that when a ball is hit down the middle, they both automatically turn and say 'yours.' You always want to entice your opponents to try those difficult, low percentage shots to your outside," continues Braden.

"Pros will only drive the alleys if they think their opponent is breaking too early for a ball down the center (poaching) or if they want to keep them from overplaying the middle."

At the Feet

This can be a difficult shot for some players to embrace because it is the polar opposite of the "hit 'em where they ain't" approach many of us have been taught. However, the fact is, quite often the best shot is one hit right at your opponent's feet.

I can't tell you how many times I've seen a player with an easy, high volley make an error because they attempted to "hit 'em where they ain't" by angling the ball off the court instead of simply hitting right down at their opponents' feet.

Of course the goal is not to hit your opponent but rather to force them into an error or weak reply. If they are able to get your low shot back, they'll have to hit "up" and most likely their return will be an easy sitter for you to drive back down the middle or at their feet again.

A brief word about hitting the opposing player: more often than not, when a player gets hit, it's their own fault. They're either not in the right position or not paying attention.

Words From the Wise

USPTA pro Will Hoag says that "One reason players make errors on the forehand volley is that their wrists don't stay firm during contact, resulting in misdirected shots."

"To cure this problem," says Will, "point the palm of your hitting hand in the direction you want the ball to go and freeze it there."

Competitive doubles is a fast, aggressive game where quite often the best shot is right at the opposing player so it's up to everyone on the court to remain focused and properly positioned. If you do accidentally hit someone, immediately make sure that they are okay and, in the spirit of good sportsmanship, raise your hand as a sign of apology. Be sincere but don't hesitate to go at them again.

Over Their Heads

One of the most misunderstood and under used shots in recreational tennis is the lob. Watch a lower level match and you'll see lots of lobs because the lob is the only way that players at that level are able to keep the ball in play. By using the lob, they're able to play long and enjoyable points.

Then a funny thing happens. Players get a bit better, learn to hit the ball harder and totally forget about the lob. They figure that since they are able to hit the ball hard, they should always hit the big shot. As a result, each team tries to out hit the other and their matches often become an error-fest.

Now, take a look at a match between two teams at the 4.5-to-5.0 level. What do you see? Long, exciting points with lots of lobs! These players have gotten over the ego boost of hitting that rare world-class shot, and have learned that the lob is one of the most effective weapons in the game.

When your opponents take control of the net and you are not certain that you can drive a good, low shot, put it up in the air. Force them to move back and hit an overhead, the most physically demanding shot in the game. I'd much rather have my opponents hit a winning overhead to beat me than to beat myself with a silly, unnecessary error.

"People tend to think of it (the lob) as a weakness in tournament tennis, but it's not - it's a gigantic strength," says Vic Braden. "People make fun of those players who like to throw up a lob every two or three shots, but they seem to forget that good lobbers have more trophies than any other person at the club."

Be it the lower, offensive lob used to surprise or push your opponents away from the net or the high, deep defensive lob which gives you time to recover, there is not a good team out there who does not possess and understand the benefits of an effective lob. In fact, I feel that the lob is a must-have for all doubles players. We'll look at the lob in depth in the next chapter.

Remember, down the middle, at the feet, or over the head. Hit a large majority of your shots with these tips in mind and you'll be amazed at how your team's errors will decrease and your number of wins increase.

12

Beyond the Serve

Adding special shots to your arsenal

In every doubles match, the serve and return of serve are the two most important shots in the game. They're the first two shots of every point and how well or poorly they're executed often determines which team will win the point.

However, there are other shots that you and your partner can use that will have just as much of an impact on the results of your matches. If hit correctly at the right time these secret weapons can be as devastating and deflating to your opponents as a 100 m.p.h. serve.

The Most Useful Shot in the Game

One of the things that separate 3.0 level teams from those at the higher levels is that the stronger teams make fewer errors. A large portion of errors are due to trying the wrong shot at the wrong time. Often I'll see doubles teams, on the defensive after their opponents have won that all-important race to the net, try to bail themselves out with a low percentage, power groundstroke. The result is usually an error and easy point for the opponents.

This approach is prevalent among the 3.0-4.0 set. These players, who have begun to develop strong groundstrokes, often panic when pressured and go for the great shot. The 4.5 and above teams understand that winning doubles is not about hitting a few great shots but rather a lot of pretty good ones.

These teams have moved away from the "big shot" mentality and moved toward point development. They play patient tennis, probe the opposing team for weaknesses and try to control the net. Above all, they refuse to give the other team free points.

The next time you or your partner find yourselves on the defensive, instead of trying a high-risk shot, hit your opponents a high, deep lob. This, often disrespected, shot can be a life raft for your team when you find yourself scrambling.

Hit Up

I frequently tell my students that, whenever they are out of position either relative to the court or the ball, to remember to "hit up." Put the ball back in play and force the other team to hit another shot to win the point. Remember, even the shortest, weakest lob is better than an error because by forcing your opponent to hit an extra shot you're giving them one more opportunity to miss. You'll be amazed at how often they'll accommodate you.

Chasing down lobs and hitting overheads are two of the most physically demanding and frustrating skills in the game to master. Even if your lob is put away, you've still made your opponent hit an extra shot. Plus, if you can force them to hit two or three overheads to end a point, their tongue will eventually be dragging.

An additional advantage of the lob is that it will keep a net-rusher guessing. Many "macho" men and women are stubborn and refuse to lob. Their opponents know this so they charge the net like a bull in a china shop. By throwing up the occasional lob, you're telling your net rushing opponents that they must always be aware of the possibility of a lob. With this thought in their heads, they won't charge as aggressively or get as close to the net. This then opens up the possibility of driving a shot at their feet.

Different Kinds of Lobs

There are two types of lobs—**offensive and defensive**. An offensive lob should set you up to win the point, while a defensive lob is designed to keep you in the point.

Words From the Wise

For example, your opponent hits a strong approach shot, and you have to scramble just to reach it. Rather than try a low-percentage passing shot from an awkward position on the court (and with the ball out of your strike zone) throw up a high, defensive lob and make him hit the ball to beat you.

A defensive lob might not even go over your opponent's head but by hitting it very high, preferably deep and crosscourt (the court is 6.2 feet longer crosscourt) you're giving yourself time to recover your position or even catch your breath while your opponent has to decide how to play the ball. If he goes for the overhead, he'll have a tough time, because the higher the ball has been hit, the faster it will fall, making the shot tougher to time.

> To keep opponents off balance, USPTA Pro Phil Parish tells his students to lob the first two points on their opponents serves. This not only keeps your opponents off-balance", says Phil, "it opens up the court for other returns."

More often than not, if you hit a lob high and deep enough, your opponent will be forced to let it bounce. Then he will have to back away from the net even more to either hit the overhead or play the ball back with a groundstroke. Either way, you'll have pushed him off the net and into a less threatening position, while at the same time giving yourself time to recover.

Offensive Surprise

The time to hit an offensive lob is when you're in control of your shot and a lob is the last thing your opponent's expecting. Let's say

they've come to the net behind a short approach shot. As you move forward, they're likely to anticipate a passing shot and move closer to the net. This is the ideal time to surprise them with a lob.

The offensive lob should not be hit as high as the defensive lob. It should go just over the net player's outstretched racket. This will give the ball a low bounce, making it extremely difficult for your opponents to chase down.

I frequently use the lob during the first few games of a match. I want to test my opponent's movement and overhead skills and, if I can make them hit a few overheads early in the match, I've begun the process of tiring them out. Lots of players hit strong overheads the first four or five games of the match but, after that, are so tired they can barely lift their rackets above their head.

Lob Volley

All four players are at the net, exchanging fast paced volleys. Each team is trying to inch closer and closer to the net so that they can end the point. As you move up the level ladder, you and your partner will frequently find yourselves in this exciting position.

At this intense time, if you or your partner can execute a well-placed lob volley, you'll more often than not, get your opponents scrambling.

To hit a lob volley, loosen your grip and open your racket face slightly (strings towards the sky) just before contact. Focus on scooping under the ball. This will allow you to push the ball up off your racket and over your opponent's heads.

Though it can be devastating to your opponents, a lob volley is a risky shot because, with four players up close, if you don't get it up high enough you've given your opponents an easy overhead with two very inviting targets - you and your partner.

Much like a lob or drop shot, the lob-volley requires a great deal of touch. The next time you and your partner take the practice court try this drill to develop that all-important "feel."

1. Each player stands at the center of the service line, one on each side of the net.

2. Begin a gentle, volley rally with the goal being to keep the ball in play.

3. After four volleys, each player begins moving forward.

4. The player hitting the sixth volley will then execute a lob volley.

5. Go back to the service line and repeat the sequence.

As you begin to get the feel for the shot, you can pick up the pace of your volleys. Once the lob volley is hit, you can then play out the point.

The Half-volley

A half-volley, or pick-up, is that annoying shot you have to play when a ball bounces right at your feet. You can't move forward fast enough to hit it out of the air, and it bounces too close to you to hit a proper groundstroke. It's literally half a volley and half a groundstroke.

Usually we get caught having to play a half-volley when we approach the net and our opponent drops the ball at our feet. Sometimes, however, we have to hit a half-volley when we're standing inside our own baseline and our opponent hits a deep groundstroke right at us.

Your goal when hitting the half-volley is to just get it back in play. With an extremely short backswing or no backswing at all, keep a firm wrist, bend at the knees and lower yourself to the level of the ball, keeping your racket in front of you.

As soon as the ball hits the ground, keep your racket face square or just slightly open. The feeling is that of gently lifting the ball over the net. Your stroke should be more of a push than a swing. Stay low and use a slight, and I repeat slight, upward motion.

A good exercise to practice the half-volley is to say the words "boom boom" to yourself as fast as you can when hitting the shot. This will give you a feel for the rhythm involved and will improve your timing. Don't try to hit a winner off the half-volley, just get it back and then move into the net for you next shot or back behind the baseline so you won't have to hit another one.

Words From the Wise

USPTA pro Mark Fairchilds says that "the half-volley is primarily a touch and timing shot. The feeling of the correct half-volley hit is a "bump." The bump only borrows the speed from the incoming ball and does not add speed or acceleration to the outgoing shot."

Right at You

Norm Copeland, the legendary coach of the Rollins College Tars, often said that one of the best plays in doubles is to go right at your opponent's right hip or shoulder. Norm felt that these shots would be extremely awkward for opponents to respond to.

As you move up the level ladder, and are playing with more experienced players, you'll find that more and more often, the ball will be driven right at you. It's a great strategy in that it handcuffs the player and can force either an error or weak return.

To respond to your opponent's body shot, first try to move to one side and play either a forehand or backhand volley. Sometimes you may not have the time to move so the best play is to hit a backhand volley. Keep your wrist firm and simply let the ball hit the strings. Your opponent's pace will provide all the power you need. By returning this awkward shot, you'll make your opponents hit one more ball, giving them another opportunity to hand over the point with an error.

Slice Backhand

Topspin gets all of the press today but the ability to execute a slice backhand at the appropriate time can pay big dividends during your matches.

A few of the advantages of a slice backhand are:

·   It's easy to execute. Because the slice is hit with a high-to-low racket motion, gravity works with you and helps with your swing.

·   It can be used on a ball at any height. It's especially effective on very low or very high balls.

·   If you're pulled out wide, the slice can be a solid, defensive shot that will keep you in the point.

·   When a sliced ball hits the court, its low bounce will keep the ball out of your opponent's strike zone and drive players with extreme western grips crazy.

·   When you're inside the court, you can drive a deep, low, skidding slice that will allow you to attack the net.

·   It's great for returning wide serves or for using the "chip & charge" tactic when facing a second serve.

·   Slice is also the motion from which a drop shot is born.

Whether you hit a one hand or two handed backhand, when slicing, use the continental grip. If you use a two-hander, you'll probably want to hit your slice with one hand. Though it is possible to hit a slice backhand with two hands most players find it awkward.

As you prepare your racket, turn your shoulders so that your opponent can see your back. Bring the racket back so that it is about 6 inches above the oncoming ball. Adjust your backswing lower or higher according to the height of the ball.

As the racket moves into position, open the face slightly so that your knuckles are facing towards the sky. Lock your wrist and keep your elbow tucked in towards your body so that your racket and arm form approximately a 90 degree angle.

When the time comes to swing, step into the ball and lean forward. Move your racket along a forward and slightly downward path. As you brush down the back of the ball, try to feel as if the ball is touching each one of your strings.

Many players, when beginning to slice, will swing down too severely. This causes them to, put too much spin on the ball. The result is often a soft floating ball that your opponents can eat up. Though you're swinging down, you still want to drive through the shot. Remember, it's a gradual descent.

As your racket continues down through the ball, push your non-racket arm back towards the fence behind you. This will keep your shoulders from opening up and help you hit completely through the ball. Just after impact your racket should slightly ascend. This ascension becomes increasingly more important the deeper you are in the court as it will prevent you from driving the ball down into the net.

Finally, be sure to keep your head still and eyes focused on the point of contact for a split second after you've struck the ball. Your head is the heaviest part of your body and even a slight movement can throw your stroke off.

When you venture into the world of slice, keep in mind that there are varying degrees of spin. Trial and error will help you develop the proper feel so that you can put as much (or as little) spin on the ball depending upon what you're trying to do.

You may be in for quite a few laughs when your first attempts at hitting slice come back and hit you in the chest or shoot straight up into the air. Remember, it's all part of the learning process and with practice you'll master the techniques of hitting with slice. Soon, you'll begin to see that there are more and more things you can do with the ball depending upon how much, or how little spin you apply.

Big serves, monster groundstrokes and earth shattering overheads are generally thought of as a player's most valuable weapons. However, specialty shots like the lob, half-volley, right at you and slice backhand can cause just as much, and often more, damage to your opponents.

13

More Than One Way to Win a Match

Fascinating doubles formations

One of the things that make doubles so fascinating is the many formations and strategies each team can use to break down their opponents. Most doubles points begin for both teams with one player at the net and the other at the baseline (one up, one back formation).

Once the serve is struck and the action begins, your team could stay in that position, or move into the aggressive two players at the net (both up) formation. If your find yourselves on the defensive, you might decide to move both players to the baseline (both back) formation. During the course of a long point, you may even move back and forth between these positions - several times.

In chapter 3, I set the goal for your team of playing in the two up formation every point. As I said, at the 4.0 level and above the team that controls the net wins the point approximately 85% of the time. So, owning the net is the easiest way to win doubles matches. However, it's not the only way.

The One Up and One Back Formation

This formation, shown below, is a favorite among teams at the 3.0 level and below. These players haven't yet developed the movement, technical and anticipation skills needed to be successful in the two up formation.

By having one player at the net to be aggressive and the other at the baseline to hit groundstrokes and handle lobs, they have the entire court covered. At this level, during competitive play, the one up and one back formation gives them the best chance to win.

Interestingly, I've recently seen teams on the pro tour elect to stay in the one up, one back formation from time to time. These are teams where one or both of the players have such superb groundstrokes that they're able to sacrifice the advantage of playing the net. One player stays at the baseline, ripping groundstrokes, while the other stays at the net, hoping to pick off the opponent's shot.

If you find yourself in a match where both teams prefer the one up, one back formation keep these strategies in mind:

When you're on the baseline: As you exchange groundstrokes with your opponent, your top priority is to keep the ball away from the opposing net man. He'll undoubtedly be bouncing up and down, faking and poaching, hoping to force you into nervous errors.

Ignore him. Many player's bark is worse than their bite. They may be moving all over the court but to actually poach takes a lot of guts. If he does take the plunge and actually picks off a few of your shots, then you have to make an adjustment.

Keep him honest by hitting the occasional ball down his alley, right at him or by lobbing over his head. You'll be surprised how often an active net player will retreat into a shell after having the ball driven down his alley once or twice.

When you're at the baseline, develop tunnel vision and focus solely on hitting your shots cross court and deep. This will keep your opponent pinned to the baseline and give your partner a chance to end the point with a volley.

When you're at the net: In the one up, one back formation, the net player is the key person as he is the one that can end the point with a strong volley or overhead. As the two baseline players exchange groundstrokes, follow the ball. When the ball is hit deep to your opponent, move closer to the net and think offensively. If the shot is out wide, follow it wide to protect your alley. If it's more towards the center, shift a step or two to the center and look to poach.

As your opponent prepares to hit, watch his body and racket face to determine whether he's going to lob or drive. If he's leaning forward, think drive. Move closer to the net and try to pick off the volley. If he's leaning back and you notice his racket face open up (strings facing the sky) he's likely to lob so back up a few steps.

When the lob comes, you have three options.

* Move back and try to end the point with an overhead either between your opponents or at the feet of the opposing net player.

* If you can't get back quickly enough to hit a strong overhead, bunt it deep to the baseline player and move back towards the net.

* If the lob is too deep for you to hit in the air, have no fear, your baseline partner is there to back you up. Quickly yell "yours," switch sides and move to the opposite service line. If your partner returns the lob with a strong shot you can then move back to the net. If his return is weak, he should then yell "back" and you then quickly back peddle to join him in the two back formation. Though a defensive formation, I'll soon show you how, with the proper approach, your team can often hang in and even turn around the point.

Play Defense

When you're opponent returns the ball back past you to your partner at the baseline, you now need to think defensively. Follow the ball and move back to your service line. If the ball has gone out wide to your partner, move a bit towards the center. You can judge this by paying attention to how far away from you the ball is as it goes by.

As the ball moves past you, fight the urge to look back at your partner as he prepares to hit. Focus on the opposing net player. Look in his eyes and he'll tell you what type of shot your partner has hit. When you hear your partner strike the ball and see the net player stay still, it probably means that he has no play on the shot. Immediately begin to move forward.

If his eyes widen, most likely he's going after your partner's shot. If he raises his racket, he's probably going to try to end the point with an aggressive volley. Quickly jump to the center of the court as the space between you and your partner is his likely target. You may be able to hit a reflex volley and keep your team in the point. If possible, try to return it to the player at the baseline and then advance forward to the net.

If he begins to bend and looks as though he'll have to play his shot from below the height of the net, move forward, towards him. He'll have to volley up and by moving forward, you may be able to pick off his shot. Plus, once he sees you coming at him he'll feel tremendous pressure and might even commit an error.

Both of these moves have to be made very quickly which is another reason you want to keep your head forward and your feet active when your partner is hitting. It buys you vital extra time!

As you're moving forward and back, bounce on your toes, fake and every now and then poach. By being active you'll take him out of his comfort zone and find that you can force him into many nervous errors. In the one up, one back formation an active net player can control the point without ever touching the ball.

If you and your partner currently favor the one up, one back formation, you can be successful but it's a tougher road to victory, particularly against a team that plays both up. During your lessons and practice sessions, work on your approaching and net skills.

You'll find that, as you continue to practice and improve, you'll begin to reap the benefits of the two up formation that I outlined in Chapter 3.

The Both-Back Formation

This formation is purely defensive yet, if employed correctly, there are several scenarios where it can help you to stay in and even turn around a point you seemed destined to lose:

1. When your opponents have won the race to the net and taken control of the point.

2. If your opponents are excellent serve and volley players, the receiver's partner can drop back to the baseline for the first serve.

3. If you and your partner have extremely strong groundstrokes but weak net games.

When your team elects to retreat to the both back formation, position yourselves 2-3 feet behind the baseline, standing inside the singles sideline.

Focus on hitting low and high: add a little topspin to your groundstrokes to make the ball drop below the net, forcing your opponents to volley "up".

Mix in lobs to push them away from the net. Pick on a particular player and vary your shots: two low shots to draw him closer to the net and then a lob, or vice versa, two lobs to push him back and then drive one low at his feet.

From this position, each team is waiting for the other to make a mistake. The net players are patiently hitting volleys and overheads deep back to their opponents while waiting for a ball they can put away.

The baseliners are hoping for one of three mistakes:

Words From the Wise

To slow down an attacking doubles team, Master Professional Dave Hagler tells his players to "hit one down-the-line lob return and one hard return right at the net player during your first return game.

"You'll give your opponents something to think about and you may even earn an early break."

1. A short ball which they can move up and attack.

2. An error by the net players.

3. A lob over the opponent's heads where they can move forward and take control of the net.

By mixing up their shots and, above all, being patient, the baseline team can often win points they initially seemed destined to lose.

Four Players Up

As you and your partner begin to compete at the higher levels, you'll frequently find yourselves face to face at the net with your opponents. Tennis at the 4.0 level and above is a battle for the net as both the server and receiver do all they can to join their partners up close.

When you find yourselves in this high intensity situation, you and your partner should focus on keeping your shots low and trying to move forward. Nine times out of ten, it will be the team that is better able to keep their heads together, their shots low, while at the same time moving forward, that will win the point.

As you can see, there is more then one way to skin a cat and win doubles matches. To see an easy-to-read reminder of the various formations as well as their advantages and disadvantages, go to Appendix B.

Spike Gonzales, a USPTA pro residing in Naples, FL, says, "In heated rallies with both teams trying to gain control of the net, players will often lose control and commit unnecessary errors. When the pace gets fast and furious, to help you and your partner learn to keep your cool, try this drill."

The next time you take to the practice court, play out points using just half the court (playing within the center service line and doubles line). One of you stands five feet behind the service line and hits an easily playable first ball to your partner who starts on the other side of the net five feet behind the baseline.

After the first ball, competitive play begins. Playing within the half-doubles-court boundaries, both of you try to win the point by attempting to advance forward. Points can only be scored if one of you wins the rally from inside the service line.

Play a game to 7 or 11, and then switch positions. This can be done either cross-court or down the line.

Spike emphasizes, "After each point determine what caused your error and work on improving," and points out that errors will fall into one or more of the following categories:

1.   Took your eye off of the ball

2.   Took too much backswing

3.   Didn't hit up enough to clear the net

4.   Tightened muscles

5.   Locked joints

Recognize and focus on these areas and you'll find your attacking skills improving dramatically.

14

Gut Check

Steps to handling pressure in a tiebreaker

You've battled in the hot sun for over three hours. Your team captured the first set, your opponents the second. The final set has gone back and forth and now you're tied at six games each. The match will be decided by a single tiebreaker.

The tiebreaker is the gut check for all doubles teams. Whether it is to decide the winner of a set or, as in some tournaments and USTA matches, to determine the winner of the match, the pressure is on when a tiebreaker comes into play.

When tiebreaker pressure strikes, the voices inside our heads can be as challenging as the team on the other side of the net. During a typical three set match (roughly 90 minutes), each player on the court will send themselves a little over 3000 verbal and non-verbal messages. For some players, those messages are largely negative:

- "Oh no, a tiebreaker. I haven't won one of these in ten years."

- "This is where my serve always falls apart."

- "My arm feels like it weighs 100 pounds."

- "I think I may throw up."

Winning players have learned to stop the negativity and turn their inner voice into a weapon for their team. Here are a few strategies to help you and your partner use you inner voices to give your team an edge when the pressure's on.

1. **Identify your thoughts**. Keep a small notebook with you on and off the court and, over a week, record all of your negative thoughts. At the end of the week look at the notebook and you'll be able to see how many times you put yourself down.

2. **Just say "No!"** You are the master of your thoughts and attitude. When you begin the downward slide into negativity and self abuse, take a deep breath, give yourself a gentle slap on the thigh and say to yourself, "No! I am not going to do this."

3. **Be positive**. Replace the negativity with positive, helpful, statements. For example, instead of telling yourself how much you hate tiebreakers, say something like "Seven more points and we win the set." Or, "These points are big. Play percentage tennis, hustle after every ball and refuse to miss." Shift the negative to positive and, if you say it enough, you will believe it.

4. **Observe, don't judge**. Pay attention to what's happening on the court but don't react emotionally to it. If you've missed your last three return of serves, instead of getting angry, remind yourself to shorten up on your backswing and move forward into the shot. Make the correction, tell yourself that you've "got it now," and move on to the next point.

Once you and your partner have conquered your inner games, you can now shift your attention outward. I spoke to a few of tennis' most sought after experts to get their strategies on how we can play our best when it counts the most.

Jeff Greenwald, a nationally recognized sports psychology consultant (www.mentaledge.net) and former ITF #1 world ranked player, says that the first thing is to remember that "there's a reason you're in a tiebreaker.

You've done quite a few things right, and you need to be clear on what they are right from the beginning of the tiebreaker. You may need to remind yourself to work the point, hit your forehand to their backhand, or get in your first serves to avoid having to rely on your second serve.

To improve your chance of winning a tiebreaker," says Jeff, "you need to narrow your focus considerably and remind yourself to play one point, even one shot, at a time. Isolating each point in this way will help you reduce your nervous tension and keep you focused on the task at hand—a skill that becomes even more critical in a tiebreaker when tension is typically high. The more you are able to isolate each point and be clear with your strategy, the more likely you will win the tiebreaker."

Words From the Wise

If you're one of those players that suffers from second serve "yips" USPTA Master Pro, Angel Lopez, offers the following advice:

"Three important elements to remember on the second serve are time, imagination and relaxation.

Time: Don't rush a second serve; bounce the ball a few times and make sure you're comfortable and balanced.

Imagination: Take a second to visualize the path of the ball. In your mind's eye, it should travel 3 or 4 feet above the net and land comfortably in the box.

Relaxation: Finally, relax your serving hand and exhale as you swing.

Give meditation a try

If you're like me, focusing on a single thing is a major challenge. Just the other day, I was preparing to hit a backhand passing shot when visions of Chinese food for dinner popped into my head. Needless to say, my passing shot was less than stellar.

To combat the many competing voices in my head, I've recently begun meditation practice. No, I don't sit in a dark room with lit candles and strange music in the background. I find a quite corner, sit and sink into my head for a few minutes each day.

Since beginning my practice, I've found that the battling thoughts in my head have calmed down which makes it much easier for me to focus both on and off the tennis court.

Jim Loehr, a performance psychologist who has worked with tennis stars such as Jim Courier, Monica Seles, and Arantxa Sanchez-Vicario suggests these two exercises as an introduction to meditation:

1. Lying in bed take a deep breath and extend the exhalation for as long as you can. On the exhalation say, "One," in your head and visualize the number one. On the next exhale, say and visualize "two," and so on. "You may get to 40 or 65 and then get distracted, so you have to start again," says Loehr, "but the whole point is just to learn what it is to be totally removed from distractions." It's a skill, he says, that will help you on the tennis court, and when you play other sports, but also in life.

2. Inhale to a count of four, pause briefly, and then exhale on a count of four. "You become one with your breathing," Loehr says, "you get into a rhythm that just takes over." What you learn is how it feels to be totally engaged in one thing: breathing.

"Meditation is essentially about being in the moment," says Loehr. When you can do that your tennis will move to another level.

(More info: how-to-meditate.org ; lgeperformance.com)

Tom Veneziano, a Texas based teaching pro and founder of the hugely popular Tennis Warrior System (More info: tenniswarrior. com) feels that "the key to success in the tiebreaker is to adapt a controlled aggressive approach."

"Approaching the tiebreaker with an aggressive attitude does not mean teeing off on big shots or recklessly charging the net," says Tom. "Rather, it means taking charge from a psychological standpoint.

Each point in a tiebreaker is like winning an entire game," says Veneziano. "You want to take the initiative and keep your opponent under constant pressure, but without risky play. This can be done in several ways:

1. Making sure your first serve is in. Take a little pace off the ball to do so.

2. Attacking the net at the appropriate time.

3. Take control of the pace of the match. Speed up the time in between points if your team takes the lead. Slow it down if you fall behind.

4. Be certain to get all return of serves in play.

Though sound advice for any stage of a match, this controlled aggressive approach can be particularly effective in tiebreakers. Many players, when the big moment comes, retreat into a shell and begin playing not to lose rather than playing to win. Your most successful players take a controlled aggressive approach and do as much as they can to control the outcome of the tiebreaker and the match.

"Be careful though," says Veneziano, "controlled aggressive play can easily turn into reckless pandemonium. If you find that you are missing often and becoming out of control, back off from your overly aggressive play. Remind yourself that you are attempting to keep pressure on your opponent, but at the same time not go outside your own ability or style."

Geoff Norton, one of the United States' top coaches for elite players tells his students to "become a wall for the first few points. Getting a lot of balls back in play will help you to discover if your opponent has tightened up."

Norton adds that "the tiebreaker is not the place to find a new stroke or strategy. Go with the shots that brought you to the tiebreaker. If you don't own it, you can't rent it, so stay away from it."

Tomaz Mencinger, who has been coaching nationally ranked juniors in Slovenia for the past twelve years, says that, "the tie-break will certainly be the most stressful part of the set. Mencinger, who has dedicated an entire website (More info: tennismindgame.com) to the mental game says that players should keep the following tiebreaker tips in mind:

1. Before the match

You must consider the possibility of playing a tie-break or two in your next match. If you know your opponents, then pre-match preparation should include visualization of main tactics you will have to counter and main tactics you'll play.

You should also visualize how you'll handle being ahead, falling behind as well as how you'll deal with a tied score such as 5-5 towards the end of the tiebreaker. In all situations stay positive, focus on the process (how you will play) and not on the outcome (what the score will be).

2. At 6-5 and 6-6

During the changeover at 6-5, you have time to re-assess your opponent's main tactics of the day and whether your pre-match tactical plan is a good one. While you should certainly focus on winning the game, take a few seconds to prepare for the possibility of the tie-break.

You have only 25 seconds at 6-6 to start the tiebreaker and this is when your pre-match preparation will pay-off. Find the mental state that you visualized before the match and focus on what you want to play.

3. During the tie-break

Again, your pre-match visualization should keep you on track whether you fall behind or move ahead. Re-focus immediately after mistakes, control your arousal level by taking enough time during the points and stick to the rituals of serving and returning so that pressure won't make you rush.

A tie breaker is something to be savored, not feared. To have reached a tiebreaker means that your team is playing well and close to capturing the set. During every practice session, be sure to play at least two or three tiebreakers. Start at various scores: some where you're ahead and others where your team is behind.

Once the tiebreaker starts, be up on your toes and radiate confidence. Not only will this combat your team's nerves, it will show your opponents that you're eager and ready to fight. Remind each other to narrow your focus. Play each point in a controlled, aggressive manner and, above all, keep it positive. When you do, you and your partner will tame the tiebreaker and, in the process, take down your opponents.

Note: See Appendix D for a complete explanation of how to play the various tiebreakers.

15

Tennis Suduko

Getting in your opponent's head

One of the great things about doubles at the 4.0 level and above is that it's a strategic battle. While matches at the 3.5 level and below can often deteriorate into a race to see which team misses enough shots to lose the match first, a high level doubles team will rarely beat itself.

That being the case, one of your team's biggest challenges is to solve the many strategic puzzles that your opponents bring to the match. Much like the wildly popular game Suduko, this requires a careful analysis as well as the ability to think ahead and put together a strategy for victory.

To conquer the puzzle that is the opposing team, you and your partner must begin to study them from the moment you take the court right through the end of the match. As you warm up with your respective opponents, practice these information gathering strategies:

1. Feed a ball right at their body and see which stroke they chooses to hit. This might give you an insight into which shot each player prefers.

2. Are they right or left-handed? I've lost count of the number of times I've asked this question to players after a match and they didn't know the answer.

3. Look at their net game. What grip do they use? Your best net players will use the Continental grip as it allows them to move between forehand and backhand volleys quickly as well as serve and volley more effectively. Is their volley motion short and compact or do they like to hit swinging volleys. Generally speaking, the player with short and compact volleys will be the more effective player while the opponent with the swinging volley will usually be more erratic.

4. Try to get a sense of which player is the captain of the team as he or she may very well be the stronger player. When you spin the racket, see which player calls "up or down" and makes the decision whether to serve or receive. The captain will usually be the team member that does most of the talking and tries to dictate the warm-up and pace of the match.

5. Pay attention to their grips and technique on their groundstrokes. Every grip has its advantages and disadvantages. For example, if one member of the opposing team uses a semi-western or western grip for his forehand, he'll struggle with low balls. Plus, Western grip players often are not great at the net. If he uses a Continental grip on his forehand, high bouncing balls will drive him nuts.

   If one player has a two-handed backhand, he'll probably be able to hit the ball a bit harder as well as execute some difficult angles. Wide balls and shots into the body will be tough for him.

6. Be certain to test both players' overheads. Feed them a lob and then a low volley so that you can get an idea of how well they move back for the overhead and then moves back in for the next shot.

7. Pay attention to their body language. Do they hustle after the ball or do they appear lazy? Do they seem relaxed or nervous? How do they handle the inner game? Does one member of the team appear to get angry when he misses a warm up ball?

Keep in mind that many teams, in an attempt to set an intimidating tone, will begin ripping the ball right off the bat. Their strategy is to win the warm up and, in the process, gain a psychological edge when the real contest begins.

Don't fall for their folly. The Williams sisters or Bryan brothers are not on the other side of the net preparing to rip you to shreds. Once the match begins, they'll come down to earth.

Once the Match Begins

During the first two or three games, keep the ball in play and focus on playing classic "percentage" doubles:

* A high percentage (70%) of first serves in

* Control the net

* Get in at least one poach each service game

* Attack your opponent's second serve

* Hit a high number of shots low and down the middle

* When in trouble, lob!

Use the first few games to settle into a comfortable rhythm as well as continuing to check out your opponents. As the match progresses, gather information and make strategic adjustments. Keep your cool and remember that, no matter what they're throwing at you, there is an answer. Here are six likely scenarios you'll face and a few tips for each.

If your opponents:

Are strong serve and volley players: Focus on returning low to the server's feet and lobbing over his partner's head. If that doesn't work, move to the both back formation on the first serve.

Prefer the one up, one back formation: Get to the net and look to execute shots between the two players and at the opposing net player's feet.

Have one team member that is much stronger than the other: Pick on the weaker player. Make him hit virtually every shot.

Both have excellent lobs: Don't abandon your net rushing strategy. When you come in, position yourselves around the service line so that you can handle the lobs.

Never lob: The match should be yours. Both you and your partner should position yourselves three feet away from the net and have a field day putting away volleys.

Are killing you with their cross-court angled return of serves:

Focus on serving down the middle to make the angle more difficult to achieve. You can also play the Australian formation which will take the receiver out of his rhythm.

These are just a few examples of what to look for when you analyze your opponent's games. Your goal as a team is to pay attention to everything. The more you can learn, the better you'll be able to devise your game plan. More often than not, at the higher levels, **it's not the team that hits the better shots that wins the match - it's the team that hits the smarter shots!**

16

Getting Better After the Match

How we did it for Jim & Susie

To help your team continue to improve, it's a great idea after every match, to find a quiet spot where you and your partner can sit down and discuss the match. Do this as soon as possible while things are still fresh in your mind. An exception to this might be if your team has just lost an emotional heartbreaker. If emotions are running high, go your separate ways for a few hours and, when enough time has passed, come back and enjoy a beverage together and talk about the match.

Do a team analysis of the match from a technical, strategic, emotional and physical perspective.

Technically speaking, take a look at how your shots held up during the pressure of the match. Ask each other questions such as:

1. Were we both able to get a large percentage of first serves in the court?

2. How well did we return serve?

3. Were our volleys consistent and penetrating?

4. How about overheads? Were we both solid when lobbed?

5. Was Mike's slice backhand return of serve that he's been working on effective?

From a strategic perspective, look at things such as:

1. Were we able to force our opponent's to play our game or did they dictate the match?

2. Did the serving and volley strategy work well for our team?

3. Were we able to execute at least one successful poach each service game?

4. What adjustments did we make after we lost the first set?

5. Was the Australian formation we decided to try effective when we used it?

How did your team perform from an emotional standpoint?

1. Were we able to keep our emotions in check or did we let things get to us?

2. When we got down a break, were we able to pick each other up and stage a comeback or did the team collapse?

3. When the big points arrived, how did we respond? Did we rise to the occasion or did we choke? If nerves got the better of you when it counted most, you need to recreate that pressure when you play your practice matches.

A great way to simulate match-pressure is to grab another team, take to the practice court, and play practice sets from specific scoring situations. Here are two of my favorites:

1. To help your team get used to the pressure, play a set where each player gets only one serve and each game begins at 30-40. Having to hit a second serve on break point is one of the greatest pressures you'll face during our matches.

2. Play a practice set where the team that wins each game gets a point advantage in the next game. If your team is serving and wins the first game, your opponents serve the second down 0-15. If you win that game, your partner then serves the third game with a lead of 30-0. If your opponents fight back and win that game, they then serve with a lead of 15-0. It's a great exercise which will teach your team how to fight from behind.

How did the team hold up physically?

1. Were you both able to get to the net as quickly in the third set as you did in the first?

2. Did your overheads, the most physically demanding shot in the game, hold up as well in the third set as the first?

3. Did your shoulders tire in the third set? How about your legs?

Keep in mind that even the slightest physical decline can affect your team's performance. If fatigue causes you to be a step slower getting to the net or moving back for an overhead it can mean the difference between hitting an effective shot, and committing an error.

You may have the best strokes at the club but if you don't have the energy to get to the ball or strength to swing the racket your beautiful strokes become useless. Most recreational players, at all levels, could benefit from additional exercise. In chapter 18, I'll give you some doubles specific fitness tips.

Keep a Record

While talking about your match is always helpful, being able to have a reference to look at can give your team some tremendous insights that you might not have remembered or been aware of.

Taping and charting are two other ways to record your match. Videotaping is great because you can do it by yourselves. Charting can also be helpful when you watch team members or the pros play matches.

The camera doesn't lie

The best way to shoot a tennis match is to set up a camera behind, and above, the court. If that's not feasible, place the camera on a tripod and shoot through the back fence. Be sure that the camera captures the entire court as it's important that you see how your team moves and reacts from all areas of the court as well as how you respond to where your opponents are positioned.

When you sit down to watch the tape, pretend you're John McEnroe the tennis commentator, and tell it like it is. Look at each player's strokes and movement and pay attention to what worked and what didn't.

If possible, have your pro watch the video with you as he or she will be able to spot specific areas of your game that may not be apparent to you and your partner. If you play on a team, you'll probably have a pro working with you that will be at your matches and available to watch your video.

As you watch your match video, pay attention to these important areas:

1. **Which team is controlling the majority of points?** Remember, the team that controls the net controls the point. Are you and your partner winning the race to the net or are you getting caught on the defensive?

2. **Are both of you mixing up your serves?** Many players fall into the pattern of serving to the same spot, time after time

and then don't understand why their opponents are ripping their returns past them.

3. **Are you both being active at the net, poaching and faking?** Remember, high level teams try to get in at least one poach each game.

4. **How was the team's movement?** Are you moving up and back as well as side to side together or is one player breaking down and opening up holes in the court?

5. **Are you attacking your opponent's second serves and moving in to the net or hanging back at the baseline?** A missed first serve by your opponent is usually an invitation for your team to take control of the net. Return cross-court and move forward!

6. **Is the team being patient and developing points or panicking under pressure and going for the "big" shot?** Winning points with one big shot is a tough road to hoe. Develop your points with 2-3 shot combinations and gradually break down your opponent's games and their spirit. Patience will eliminate most of your unforced errors. If you or your partner are off balance either relative to the ball (too close or far away) or the court (well behind the baseline or off to the side) remember, don't try to end the point with a spectacular (low percentage) winner. Lob the ball back and give your opponent another opportunity to make an error.

Charting Your Match

Though you can devise charts to analyze your matches in any number of ways, here are two charts that we recently developed for one of our USTA mixed doubles teams, Jim and Susie. Jim had been having trouble with his serve and Susie, her return, so we put together a very simple chart for their next match that would focus in on just those shots.

Jim's Serving Statistics

A member of Jim's team watched the match and recorded a sample of his serving statistics. The first column showed the number of points Jim served. The next three columns will tell us whether he got his first serve in, his second or if he double faulted.

# Served	1st Serves in	2nd Serves in	Double fault
1	X		
2		X	
3			X
4		X	
5			X
6		X	
7			X
8			X
9		X	
10			X

Analyzing the chart you can see that, out of ten points, Jim double-faulted five times. Plus, he only got his first serve in 10% of the time! Like many players, Jim likes to go for the big bomb on his first serve. As is usually the case with this strategy, his first serve seldom went in which left him with the pressure of having to hit a second serve in the court or lose the point. Looking at his chart, we can see that, with five double faults, the pressure clearly got to him.

Our advice to Jim was to, during his next match, hit his second serve first. By taking a little pace off the ball and adding some spin, we were confident that his first serve percentage would rise and take away the pressure of having to hit so many second serves.

Here's how it went:

# Served	1st Serves in	2nd Serves in	Double fault
1	X		
2	X		
3		X	
4	X		
5			X
6	X		
7	X		
8	X		
9		X	
10	X		

Big improvement! Jim's first serve percentage jumped to 70% and he only double faulted one time! Not surprisingly, he won every game he served.

Words From the Wise

USPTA professional David Macburnie tells his students to "Think of your racket face as an extension of the palm of your hand when getting ready to hit a serve."

"By creating the perfect strike zone with your palm on the ball, you'll gain much better control over your serve as well as minimize errors into the net."

Susie's Return of Serve

Susie had been struggling with her return of serve so we devised the chart below to help her get a clearer picture of what was happening.

The first column recorded each return of serve she hit. The next two columns told us whether she returned a first serve or second. The fourth column told us if she failed to return the serve. If an F1 was placed in the fourth column, it means the error was forced on the first serve. If there was a U2, then the error came on the second serve. We used the letter "U" to signify that the error was unforced.

ROS	1st serve	2nd serve	Error
1	X		
2			U2
3			U2
4			U2
5	X		
6			F1
7			U2
8			U2
9	X		
10			U2

Out of ten points, Susie missed seven returns of serve. Of those seven, six returns were missed off of her opponent's second serve. Looking at the statistics, we came to the conclusion that Susie was being too aggressive when facing a second serve. This is a common scenario for all of us:—our opponents miss their first serve and we begin foaming at the mouth in anticipation of their weaker second. The weaker serve comes in, we take huge swing and deposit the ball into the back fence.

We suggested to Susie that, when faced with a second serve, to slow down, hit a medium paced return cross-court and then advance to the net. The statistics from her next match show a huge improvement.

ROS	1st serve	2nd serve	Error
1	X		
2		X	
3		X	
4		X	
5			F1
6		X	
7		X	
8		X	
9	X		
10		X	

Whether your team won or lost your last match there is always something to be gained. Study the information from your team, chart and/or video analysis. Be honest with yourself, each other, and insist that your coach do the same. Keep in mind that the purpose of them all is to help your team improve so take the information, head to the practice court and you'll be well on your way to the next level.

17

Downward Facing Dog & More

Fun doubles practice routines

"Failing to prepare is preparing to fail." Legendary basketball coach John Wooden used these words to inspire his UCLA Bruins teams to 10 national championships in the 60s and 70s. A master of preparation and focus, Wooden believed that basketball games were won and lost on the practice floor. I believe coach Wooden would have made one heck of a tennis coach.

Serious doubles teams recognize the value of focused practice sessions towards their match preparation. At least once a week, you and your partner should walk onto the court with a specific plan and set of drills that will allow you to hit as many balls as possible and work on your doubles skills.

When you step onto the practice court, commit to having the same focus and intensity that you would if you were playing a tournament final. Chase down and hit every ball with energy and a purpose. Here's a sample one hour practice session that will help you and your partner prepare for any match. Be sure to take a basket or several cans of balls to the court to minimize pick-up time.

S-t-r-e-t-c-h!

Before you begin to hit balls, jump rope, do some jumping jacks, run in place, anything to break a light sweat followed by some light yoga stretching.

Andrea Lankester, a certified yoga instructor in Wilton, Connecticut and a 3.5 level tennis player, suggests the following poses for an all-body stretch:

1. Downward Facing Dog

Knees straight, heels touching or reaching toward ground, waist long, lower ribs centered, shoulder blades moving toward pelvis.

2. Warrior

Back shoulder open, torso vertical, back leg moving away from center, front leg to 90 degrees, knee over ankle.

3. Chair Pose

Shoulder blades firm against back and moving toward pelvis, natural curve in lower back, shins moving forward, heels grounded - great for Achilles.

4. Triangle Pose

Upper chest open, lower ribs even, knees straight not locked.

5. Eagle Pose

Smart Warm-up Shots

Once you're warm and stretched, use the first 20 minutes on court to warm up all of your shots in the following manner.

1. **Mini-tennis,** inside the service lines. 2 minutes

2. **Full-court rally,** lengthening your strokes. 2 minutes

3. **Crosscourt forehands.** 2 minutes

4. **Crosscourt backhands.** 2 minutes

5. **Down-the-line forehands.** 2 minutes

6. **Down-the-line backhands.** 2 minutes

7. **Reflex volleys** from service lines. 2 minutes

8. **Overheads/lobs**: Player at the baseline hits only lobs; player at the net returns the lob with controlled overheads back to the player at the baseline. Switch after 2 minutes.

9. **Serves**: Serve to both boxes. 4 minutes

Now that you're fully warmed up you're ready to pick up the pace and focus on some more doubles specific exercises starting with what I like to call:

The "Volley Games"

I'm a lucky guy in that my partner, on and off the tennis court, for nearly 30 years has been my wife Kelley. In addition to putting up with me, Kelley is also a great tennis player.

We began doing "the volley games" in college and thirty years later they're still one of our favorite drills. The volley games are a series of eight, doubles oriented exercises. Here's how we do it. We position ourselves as shown below.

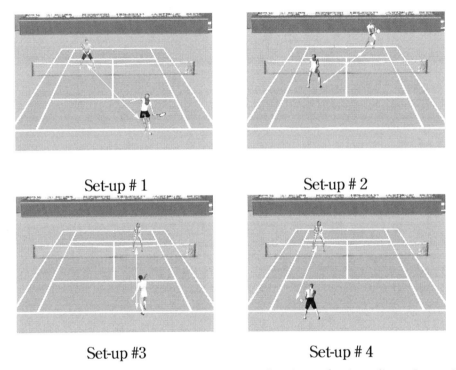

Set-up # 1   Set-up # 2

Set-up #3   Set-up # 4

In the first set-up, I'm at the net and Kelley is at the baseline. One of us feeds a ball to the other and we then play out the point, using just half the court. Alleys count. When one of us reaches 11 points, the game is over. Kelley then comes to the net (on the same side of the court), I move to the baseline, and we play again.

After the second game is completed, we move to set-up # 2 and again play two games to eleven, one with each of us at the net and the other at the baseline. Then we play two games from set-ups 3 & 4 as shown.

By the time we've gone through all eight games, Kelley and I will have had a great, doubles oriented, workout. We've practiced our volleys, overheads, groundstrokes and lobs. The "volley games" allow us to work on all of our doubles shots except the serve and return of serve which brings us to our last drill.

One on One Doubles

A fabulous new game has hit the tennis scene and it's called One on One Doubles. Developed by Ed Krass, One on One Doubles (More info: oneononedoubles.com) is a great way for players to work on their doubles skills. Here's how it works.

You and your partner play a match against each other (8 game set, 10 game set, or 2/3 sets) where you alternate points from the deuce court to the ad court. All points are played crosscourt with the alley included.

Words From the Wise

Joel Drucker, author of "Jimmy Connors Saved My Life" says that "When Connors practiced, the emphasis was on quality over quantity. That meant going for every ball on one bounce, playing balls that were out of the court, constantly moving his feet.

You would never, ever see Connors stop in the middle of a rally, pick up a ball that bounced past the baseline and starts the rally again", says Drucker. "Instead, he'd play balls from all corners, always moving. Rarely was he on-court longer than 90 minutes at a time. Rather than leave a court tired, he left it eager."

Draw a line, or place a rope, through the middle of the court from the center service line to the middle of the baseline. See below.

The player serving must serve and volley on both first and second serves. Half-volleys are permitted. The returner can stay back or come into the net. This is a great drill which allows both you and your partner to hit all of the game's shots: the serve, return of serve, first volley, half-volley, drop volley, lob, overhead and groundstrokes.

Cool down by walking around the court 2-3 times and then repeat the Yoga poses.

Take this practice plan to the court and adjust the time to suit your needs. If, in your last match, you served great but your forehand gave you fits, spend additional time on your forehand and cut out the serving.

Playing competitively is certainly a lot of fun but never forget that most matches are won and lost on the practice court. Sit down with your partner and develop a practice program that will allow you to work on all aspects of your doubles game. Commit to "practicing" at least once a week and you'll soon find that your doubles has moved to a whole new level!

Love Practice Drills?

Here are two more great practice games from two of the top pros in the business, Ken Dehart and Dr. Louie Capp.

1. Doubles My Way

"Most club players will play against the same players week after week and their games stagnate," says Dehart. "This game will invigorate their weekly play."

Each player gets to choose the rules for the next 4 games:

* One serve only

* Receiving team must lob the serve return

* Serving team must play Australian Formation

* All 4 players start on the baseline and must come to the net with the serve and return

* The ball cannot bounce on the court after the serve

* Players can only win points when serving. Lose your service point and the other team now serves

* Serving team must play in the "I" formation

"Playing Doubles My Way," says Ken, "will help your team experience new formations and styles of play that will keep those weekly games exciting and develop more options when they play league matches."

2. Dingles (not singles, the "D" stands for doubles)

"Dingles," says Dr. Capp, is a great drill to help players improve their concentration skills as well as force them to be aggressive and come to the net to play the point out.

Here's how it works:"

Four players will begin to rally using two balls. They can rally either down the line or cross court. When one ball is missed either into the net, wide or long, one of the players immediately shouts "DINGLES" and everyone has to come to the net and play the point out. After a predetermined number of points (let's say 7) everyone makes a clockwise rotation so all positions are covered.

18

Fit to Fight

Smart exercises for winning doubles

Today's doubles is a fast paced game that demands explosive movements, quick reflexes, balance, strength and flexibility. During a typical point at the 4.0 level, you could easily find yourself doing 3-5 sprints, several quick lunges to the side and having to bend and raise your knees 5-6 times while attacking and defending the net.

Plus, you'll need to react to balls that are sometimes moving at over 100 m.p.h, balance yourself to execute a controlled stroke and then quickly recover to get ready for another bullet by your opponents. For your team to compete at its best, over the course of a long match, both players need to be at their physical peak.

In addition to an overall fitness regimen that encompasses strength, flexibility, endurance and nutrition, doubles players should also pay special attention to their legs, balance, reflexes, core and vision.

Tennis is Not a Hitting Game, It's a Moving Game.

Players with beautiful strokes may be pretty to look at but those strokes are absolutely useless if the player can't get into position to hit them. Doubles is largely a legs driven game.

Whether it's jumping up for a serve or overhead, bending low to reach a volley or exploding forward into a return, strong legs are a must for all doubles players. Though you won't have to move far, you'll need to explode to the ball, recover quickly and explode again, often several times a point.

Try a Cardio Tennis Class: Conducted on a tennis court by certified instructor, Cardio Tennis is a fabulous training tool for doubles players. Each class includes a short warm-up, a cardio workout, where you're moving and constantly hitting tennis balls, and a cool down phase.

Adding Cardio Tennis to your training program is guaranteed to improve your endurance, agility and reflexes. More information on Cardio Tennis classes in your area can be found at cardiotennis.com.

Here are four of my favorite exercises guaranteed to put a spring in your step.

1. **Windshield Wiper Movement Drill:** Glen and Henry stand five feet from the net, Glen on the ad side singles sideline, Henry on the center line separating the service boxes. Glen says "Go" and then both players quickly move to the right. When Glen reaches the center line and Henry the singles sideline, they bend low and execute a forehand volley.

   Then, both players quickly move back to their starting line and execute another practice volley. The players move back and forth in this manner until each has hit ten practice volleys. Rest for 30 seconds and then switch sides. This is a fabulous drill for practicing the side to side movement at the net. It will also make your legs burn.

2. **Up and Back Movement Drill:** Glen and Henry now position themselves at the net, in the center of the service box. Henry says "Go" and they both sprint forward and touch the net with their racket. They then move back and execute a practice overhead. Then, both players quickly sprint back to the net and repeat the sequence ten times. Rest 30 seconds and then go again.

3. Single Leg Jumps

Balance yourself so that you're on your right leg. Slowly, bend so that you lower yourself into a squat position (making sure to keep your knee behind your toes) and then, using your arms, explode up off your leg and jump as high as you can. Come down gently on your right leg and then repeat 5 times. Rest 30 seconds and then repeat. Do two sets and then switch sides.

4. Jump Squats

Begin with your feet shoulder-width apart. Grab a light dumbbell in each hand and hold it at shoulder height, palms facing forward. Keeping your chest lifted and chin up, slowly bend into a squat position (making sure to keep your knees behind your toes) until your thighs are parallel to the floor. Jump straight up and land softly. Repeat 5 times. Rest 30 seconds and then repeat. Do two sets and gradually increase the weight as you get stronger.

It's a Game of Steps, Not Strokes

A tennis player's strokes get all the publicity yet, at the end of the day, tennis is not a game of strokes, it's a game of steps.

Ken DeHart, says that "player's strokes may all look the same but the effort put into getting into position to execute the stroke often divides the skill levels. The number of times your feet touch the court after you contact the ball and until you contact it again will often decide the level of player."

Ken offers the following comparison:

Pros average 10-12 steps between each shot they hit.

College players average 8-10 steps between each shot they hit.

5.0-4.5 level players average 6-8 steps between each shot they hit.

Words From the Wise

Trainer Doug Spreen, who has worked with elite athletes such as Andy Roddick, loves to have his players hit the hills. "Running hills builds incredible leg strength," says Doug.

"Running uphill forces you to work harder than you will on the court. It trains your body to the rhythm of playing a tough point, resting for a short period, and then doing it all over again,"

Spreen suggests mixing up the distances ranging from 50 to 200 meters, followed by a walk back down before running up again.

4.0-3.5 level players average 4-6 steps between each shot they hit.

2.5-3.0 level players average 2-4 steps between each shot they hit.

The next time you and your partner take to the practice court, commit to taking as many steps as possible to, and in-between, all of your shots. Make a game out of it. As you rally back and forth, each player gets a point for every step they take moving to their shots and, as they're waiting for, their next shot. At the end of the rally, the player with the most points (steps) wins.

Strengthen your legs and master the split-step and I think your team will find that your strokes, and number of wins, will improve dramatically.

Note: Ken Dehart is one of the few professionals in the world to be certified as a Master Professional by both the Professional Tennis Registry and the United States Professional Tennis Registry, Ken is also a motivational speaker, USA High Performance Coach and National Cardio Tennis Trainer. His website (More info: kendehart10s.com) has a fabulous tips and strategies page.

Balance to Win

Corey Smith, a personal trainer at The Sportsplex Club in Bethel, CT, says that " In a high intensity doubles match, you'll constantly be moving forward and backward as well as side to side. The ability to gain, and regain your balance during several direction changes will determine how effectively you're able to not only execute your shot but recover and prepare for the next."

Corey, who has been training elite athletes for over twelve years says the following exercises can be used to improve your balance. Both require equipment that are readily available in most gyms.

1. Using a mini-trampoline, stand on one leg and gently bounce up and down. As you begin to get more comfortable, grab a medicine ball and slowly toss and catch it as you move up and down. Do 10 repetitions and then switch legs. As you progress find a partner and toss the medicine ball back and forth while bouncing on one leg. This requires even more muscles to fire to create stability and balance.

2. Reebok makes a fabulous product called the Reebok Core Board (More info: reebok.com). Bosu Balls (More info: bosu. com) are also a popular balancing device used by Elena Dementieva. Balance yourself on the Core Board or Bosu Ball, hold a light medicine ball and draw the letters of the alphabet in the air. Bend your knees to hit the baseline of the letter and reach as high as possible for the top of the letter.

   "As you move through both of these exercises", says Corey, "you'll find that the constant adjustments you're forced to make to maintain your balance will not only make your legs and core stronger, they'll help you gain and regain your balance during those intense rallies up close."

Reflexes

Quick reflexes are what separates the doubles players from the pretenders. A great tool to improve your reflexes is the "Z Ball (More info: mansionselect.com).

This training aid is specially designed so that, when it lands it will bounce in unpredictable directions. Stand a few feet away from a wall, throw the "Z Ball" against the wall, let it bounce and then try to catch it.

This is a great drill to improve your reaction time, hand-eye coordination and agility. Plus, it's a lot of fun. It also comes with a fabulous video that outlines many drills to improve your reflexes.

Keep Your Core Strong

High level doubles requires a great deal of intense twisting, turning, lunging and reaching. To be able to continually repeat these movements over the course of a long match demands a strong core – legs, hips, low back, abdominals and obliques. Here are two exercises Corey recommends to firm you up fast.

Medicine Ball Mini Tennis: A favorite of tennis legend Pete Sampras, this drill is a variation of the popular mini-tennis game. Stand at the service line on your side of the court and your practice partner does the same on the other. Instead of rallying with a tennis ball, you and your partner throw a medicine ball back and forth. Keeping the ball inside the four service boxes, you can catch it in the air or let it bounce. You can even play out points. Be sure, with each throw, to rotate your shoulders and hips to simulate forehands and backhands.

Medicine Ball Lunge and Twist: This is an exercise that not only strengthens you from head to toe, but also improves your balance. Holding a medicine ball with both hands in front of your chest, step one foot backward. Bend both knees to create 90 degree angles. As you bend your knees twist the torso and shoulders to drop the ball down to the outside of the front leg.

Rewind the motion by untwisting the torso, bringing the ball back to starting position and stepping the back leg forward. Do 10-15 repetitions on each leg. Increase the weight of the medicine ball and the number of repetitions as you become stronger.

Get your Eyes in Shape

A tennis ball will often be moving back and forth across the net at speeds of over eighty miles per hour. If your team can pick up the ball faster and more effectively than your opponents you'll be at a tremendous advantage during those fast, up close, exchanges.

Dr.'s Donna Mackler and John Peroff in the book "Fit to Play Tennis" discuss three types of vision that tennis players need and offer exercises to improve each:

Dynamic Visual Acuity "involves the ability to maintain clear vision while the athlete and/or the target (ball) is in motion." To improve your visual acuity, the doctors prescribe this exercise:

"While watching television, switch to the scrolling stock quotes and read out loud the numbers and letters on the screen. Try to do this task while running on the spot or doing dynamic exercises such as bouncing on a mini-trampoline."

Peripheral Awareness "relates to the ability to concentrate on the ball and know where the court lines are at all times." Here's a great exercise to improve your peripheral vision: "While walking, look straight ahead and see how much detail you can pick out from the periphery."

Depth Perception "is the ability to precisely judge the position of objects. Timing of the swing depends upon fine depth perception and relies on the ability of the brain to detect the subtle differences in information coming from each of the two eyes. Good depth perception is necessary for accurate shot placement, evaluation of opponents' position on the court, and evaluating whether the ball is in or not."

This exercise is one I've done for years to improve my depth perception. Hold a pen, an arm's length away, in front of you. Focus your vision on the tip of the pen for 5 seconds. Then, shift the focus of your vision to an object that is farther away for 5 seconds. Go back and forth between your pen and a distant object ten times.

Note: With all of these exercises, begin slowly and don't rush the movements. As always, be sure to check with your physician before beginning any new exercise regimen.

In Times of Injury, Listen to Your Body and React Quickly

Injuries are a part of an active life and though we may try to deny it, we're all only human, so from time to time we're going to break down. When that inevitability occurs, your number one concern becomes minimizing its effects.

Chuck Giordano, a licensed Physical Therapist and Strength and Conditioning Specialist from Ridgefield, CT says, "Most tennis-related injuries can be treated by remembering the acronym RICE, which stands for rest, ice, compression and elevation.

Most common injuries are related to a minor disruption of soft tissue (muscles, ligaments and tendons)," says Chuck. "When a trauma occurs to these tissues, cells and small blood vessels rupture leading to swelling. If you can minimize that swelling immediately after the injury, you'll have much less pain and recover faster."

"Pain is your body's way of telling you something is wrong and should not be ignored," cautions Giordano. "Take a few days off, apply a cold pack directly to the painful and swollen area and elevate it above the level of your heart. Studies have shown that by applying the RICE method immediately following an injury can reduce time lost to injury by 50% when compared to doing nothing at all. Gentle active range of motion within a pain free range is also usually helpful. The motion promotes normal circulation and helps prevent stiffness and loss of motion."

Giordano, who has treated weekend warriors as well as elite athletes such as James Blake, says that "most tennis-related injuries are minor and can be treated with rest and a little common sense. However, if your pain doesn't go away after a week to ten days, comes on suddenly or is severe, see your doctor." (More info: ridgefieldphysicaltherapy.com)

How Fit are You?

Legendary fitness trainer Pat Etcheberry, who has worked with stars such as Andre Agassi, Justine Henin, Pete Sampras, and Jim Courier, has developed several tests to help players assess their level of fitness. Here are two of his favorites:

Fitness Test # 1: Measures Quickness, Recovery & Stamina

1. Stand in the center of the service box.

2. Quickly move from side to side, touching the singles sideline and then the center service line with your racket. Continue back and forth for 30 seconds, keeping count of the number of lines you touch.

3. Rest for 30 seconds and then do it again. Be sure to count the number of lines you touch.

4. Rest for another 30 seconds, then do the drill for one final 30-second period, again counting each line you touch.

You should now have three set of numbers and Etcheberry says that each number provides him with an important piece of information.

The first number tells him how fast you are. The second number tells him how quickly you recover after a long point. The final number measures your stamina. Your goal should be to get around same number on each round.

To see where you should be relative to your peers, find the age closest to yours and compare your score to the average listed under your gender.

Age	Male	Female	Age	Male	Female
PRO	38	33	18	35	31
10	29	25	21	36	32
12	31	27	40	34	28
14	33	29	50	29	25
16	34	30	60	26	22

Fitness Test #2: Measures Leg Strength

Have two friends hold a jump rope 18 inches off the ground. Then, hop back and forth over the rope for 20 seconds. 2 sets with a 2 minute rest in-between. Take the best score of the two.

Peer Comparison

Age	Male	Female	Age	Male	Female
PRO	48	43	16	44	29
10	37	32	18	45	40
12	40	35	21	46	41
14	42	37	40	42	37

These results are neither good nor bad. They are simply a starting point. Go from here, consult your pro or a personal trainer, and develop an on and off court training program to improve your fitness. Test again in a few weeks and you should see that you are well on your way to the next level. "If you can handle these tests," says Etcheberry, "you'll be ready for any match."

If a pro or personal trainer is not readily accessible or within your budget, you can have Pat Etcheberry in your living room. He has produced a fabulous series of fitness DVDs called "The Etcheberry Experience." You can do the same drills that Pete Sampras, Andre Agassi, Justine Henin and Jelena Jankovic and many others use to get themselves into peak form. (More info: etcheberryexperience.com)

19

Thriving in the World of Social Doubles

Etiquette for the social doubles scene

You've just arrived home from a tough week at the office and your loving spouse greets you at the door with a kiss and your tennis racket. "Remember honey? Tonight's the mixed scramble at the club. Hurry up and get your shorts on."

A strong blow to the stomach best describes the feeling that comes over you. You're tired and just want to have dinner, melt into your favorite chair and watch the Tennis Channel. Plus, you're a "serious" player and an evening of "social" tennis is as appealing to you as an old can of balls.

Your wife senses your reaction and disappointment swims into her eyes. Recently bitten by the tennis bug, she takes weekly lessons, has just learned to serve and can't wait to get to the courts. You recover quickly, push a smile onto your face and reply, "Great. Just give me a minute to get changed."

Whether you're a serious competitive player, weekend warrior or have just learned which end of the racket to hold, social tennis events can not only be a great deal of fun, they can also help your game. Here are five strategies to help you get the most out of your next social tennis experience.

1. Arrive on time

Though you are coming to a social event, it is not a cocktail party where it's fashionable to be late. More than likely, the pro has arranged a game for you right from the start and if you saunter in twenty minutes late, you'll have rudely kept others waiting. If you're going to be late, notify the person running the event so they can keep you out of the first round.

2. Come prepared to be social

Whether you're at the scramble by choice or out of marital guilt, you're there so you might as well enjoy yourself. View the event as a chance to unwind from the stresses of the week and spend time in a relaxed and casual atmosphere. Look to meet new people. Who knows, you might even find another competitive player that you can begin to work out with or a new business contact.

3. Adjust your level of play to the others on the court

During a typical four round tennis social, ideally, you'll play a round with stronger players, one with weaker players and two at your level. Learning to adjust to each will enable you, and the others on the court, to have a great time.

Yes, I know you're the club champion, have won your last six league matches and finally beaten your boss but a social event is not the place to display your greatness. If you find yourself on the court with weaker players, let the air out of your ego.

Take down the pace. Keep the ball in play and, every now and then, set up your opponents for an easy put-away. It will make them and, believe it or not, you feel good.

Over and above everything else, encourage the other players on the court. Don't coach them unless they ask.

If you happen to be the weak link on the court, now's the time to raise your game. You'll be nervous but that's okay. Keep your feet active, focus on the ball and prepare your racket as quickly as possible. Be sure to breathe in and, just as you make contact with the ball, breathe out. This will help push the nerves aside.

Fight the urge to try shots you don't own at paces you can't control. Chase down every shot and limit your unforced errors. The key is to focus on getting lots of balls back. Show them that you're not going to roll over just because they're "supposed" to be better than you. Have fun hanging in there.

If you find yourself on the court with players of equal ability then you can let it all hang out. Yes, it's social but if everyone is at the same level then the game can become a bit more spirited. Play hard and go for your shots.

4. Surviving a tennis snob*

We've all had our experiences with the dreaded tennis snob. You arrive at the social event, excited to have some fun. After a brief warm-up, the pro gathers everyone together to announce the pairings for the first round.

"On court # 2, Anne (you) will play with (snob) Sally against Joan and Jane."

The exaggerated rolling of her eyes and dropping of her shoulders gives you a clue that Sally is less than thrilled with the pairing. You step onto the court and instantly become the beneficiary of free instruction. You're told where to stand, how to hit and above all to "stay out of my way."

The fun continues as the match begins: she groans when you miss an overhead, looks as if she's been punched in the stomach when you double fault and is quite adept at convincing your opponents, and everyone else at the event, that her errors are directly related to your weak play.

The fact is tennis snobs are everywhere and can ruin an otherwise enjoyable tennis experience. Don't let them. Their attitude is their issue, not yours. When the snob picks you as their target, fight the urge to practice your new serve over their head and employ one of these anti-snob strategies:

- **Agree with the snob.** When his words or body language scream out "How could you miss that easy shot" agree with him and say "You're right, I should have had it." By agreeing, you'll immediately diffuse the situation.

- **Ignore the snob.** The snob can only get to you if you let him. Ignore his glare and move on to the next point.

- **Laugh.** The next time the snob makes you want to smack them over the head with your racket, smile and let out a small laugh. Steve Wilson, founder of the World Laughter Tour Inc., an organization that promotes therapeutic laughter, says that "Under acute stress, the two hemispheres of the brain become disconnected. Laughter works as a relaxation response and calms the system. It's very powerful," says Wilson

5. Shut off your cell phone

Yes, it is a "social" event but it's still rude to keep the other players waiting while you talk on your phone. Federer, Nadal and McEnroe are not calling to see if you'd like to be their fourth and Maria Sharapova is not checking in for help with her backhand. Leave the number of the club with your family or babysitter. If there is an emergency, you can be reached via the front desk.

If you are playing at a facility where there is no receptionist, leave your cell phone on, but put the ring function on the silent mode. Check it at every changeover if you must.

What to do if you think your opponents are cheating

You saw the ball hit the line but your opponents call the ball "out." What do you do?

Bad line calls are always a sensitive issue. It could be an honest mistake or perhaps your opponent wants the ball to be out so badly that he actually sees an in ball as out. Or, sadly, the other team might be cheating intentionally. Nevertheless, you and your partner must first keep your composure.

If it's a social event, let it go. Finish the round and move on. If you're playing in a competitive event, where the result of the match means something, keep these tips in mind.

· The first time it happens there's not much you can do. It's their call, and the point stands. Let it slide and move on. Keep in mind that most people don't cheat and your opponents are much closer to the ball and in a better position to make the call than you. Remember that during a high level doubles match, the ball can be traveling at an exceptionally fast speed. This combined with the fact that your opponents are usually moving as they're making the call, make it easy to see how a mistake can be made. The first time it happens, give them the benefit of the doubt.

· If it happens again, and you honestly feel the call was incorrect, take a long look at where the ball bounced and ask your opponents, politely, if they're sure of their call. Don't be rude. Don't be sarcastic, and above all, don't become confrontational. If you start out attacking them, they'll get defensive and it could get ugly. Simply say, "Are you sure?" By openly questioning their call, you're letting them know that you're paying attention. Give them a chance to take a second look and, if it was an honest mistake, allow them to correct it gracefully.

· Most players are honest and will want to make certain that they get it right. Many times the player will give you the point if you thought it was in.

· Three is the magic number. If your team receives a questionable call for a third time, continue to keep your composure, but become a bit more firm. If you're in a league match or tournament, calmly walk up to the tournament desk and request a linesperson.

Most tournaments will provide you with a linesperson to settle any disputes. If you're playing a USTA match, the club can often provide an impartial person to assist with the lines. If no help is available you'll just have to deal with the bad calls and finish the match.

Don't lose your cool and let it destroy your game. A few bad calls here and there, though frustrating, probably won't alter the result of the match. For the "cheater" to be successful, he needs for you to lose your cool. Don't!

Words From the Wise

Nick Bollettieri, says that, "No matter how intense and unpleasant the sting of a cheater is, you must stay focused on what truly matters - mastering your game and using the match to improve using skills."

Above all, don't retaliate. I've seen teams who felt they were being cheated, begin to make blatant bad calls in retribution. Bad idea! Not only does this increase the tension on the court, it also takes your concentration away from your game.

Never let your opponent's behavior allow you to lose your composure and act in a way that you'll later regret. Remember, it's not about the type of person they are—it's about the type of people you and your partner are.

20

Double Your Life

Secrets of the Ageless Warriors

Several times, every year, a group of players will come up to me and say, "We just got back from a trip to Florida where we played against these old ladies (or men). They couldn't run, couldn't hit the ball but they beat the pants off of us."

Apparently, Florida is a hotbed for great, senior tennis players. The good news is you don't have to hop on a plane to join their longevity club. With the proper strategy you can continue to enjoy tennis, and improve, throughout your entire life.

At some point we're all going to feel the effects of aging. Our tennis clothes become a bit tighter, our bodies a bit rounder and the stiffness from that tough three set match lingers on and on. I'm currently recovering from my second knee surgery. Nothing major: just some wear and tear effects from nearly forty years of chasing tennis balls, running a marathon and abusing my body in many other (supposedly) healthy athletic endeavors.

My body may be pushing back a bit but I plan on playing tennis for the next fifty years. To help achieve that goal, I recently ventured to Florida to track down some of those "super seniors" and learn their secrets. I arrived at The Villages, one of the premier retirement communities in America, with a clear mission: pick the brains of the players that live there and drink from their fountain of youth.

Director of Tennis at The Villages, Tim Farwell, said that "All of our players here share some common traits that contribute to their longevity. Farwell, who himself is a top senior player in Florida says that "Above all we love tennis and are committed to a physically active lifestyle."

Here are a few of the Villager's winning secrets:

They're Students of the Game

Legendary tennis journalist, Bud Collins, often describes tennis at its best as athletic chess. Bud's right! One reason the Villagers win so many matches is that they understand the strategies of the game. Maybe they can't hit a 120 m.p.h serve but they certainly know where to place it. They also know where to position themselves to respond to their opponent's most likely return.

Take the lessons in this book and others and become a tennis aficionado. Commit to playing disciplined, percentage tennis. When you fully learn the game, it won't matter if you can't serve as hard as you once did - you won't need to. So what if you can't run as fast as you used to? You'll know where your opponent is likely to hit their shot before they do.

If you can, find a good pro and take some lessons. Look for a pro that is accredited by either of the two main teaching organizations— the Professional Tennis Registry (www.ptrtennis.org) or the United States Professional Tennis Association (www.uspta.org).

Pros with either or both of these certifications have passed rigorous on and off-court tests that cover every facet of playing and teaching the game. Go to their websites and you can find a certified professional in your area.

They Have Secret Weapons

Even the fittest seniors don't move like they once did which makes the drop shot and drop volley valuable weapons in their arsenal.

The motion for both shots are similar to scooping ice cream out of a box. It's an exaggerated slice where you bring your racket from a high to low position. At contact, you soften your grip and "scoop" under the ball. The scoop will add backspin, which slows the ball down and can even make it bounce backwards if enough spin is applied.

The closer you are to the net the better when trying the drop shot or drop volley. Remember, you have two players on the other side of the net so there's not a lot of open space. As you move closer and closer to the net, the shots becomes easier to execute plus the less time your opponents will have to react.

A key element of the drop shot is surprise so you want to make your opponent think that you're going to hit your normal groundstroke or volley. Approach the ball with your regular preparation and but instead of driving through the ball, at the last moment "scoop" under it for the drop.

Both the drop shot and drop volley are "touch" shots and require a great deal of practice to get the proper "feel." I always urge my students to play mini-tennis to help them develop the necessary touch to make the shots effective.

If your opponents happen to catch up with your drop shot, you can then put the final nail in the coffin by throwing up a lob over their heads.

They're "Techies"

I've always been amused by the "techies" of the tennis world. You know they type: they buy the latest high tech racket and string it with new age string, convinced that it will take them to the next level. I tell these players to remember that it's not the arrow, it's the Indian. My point is that a high tech racket will not make them a great tennis player.

Well, as I've gotten older I've learned that a little help from a good arrow can help.

- If your eyesight isn't what it once was, try switching to an oversized racket with a bigger sweet spot.

- When the decades take a step or two of your speed, try one of the new extra-long frames.

- If you find that your shots begin to land shorter in the court, or aren't as powerful as they once were, string your racket a few pounds looser.

- If your shoulder, elbow or wrist throbs after your matches, consider trying a racket that is easier on the arm. Most racket manufacturers have rackets designed to give you a softer feel.

- To further protect your arm, remember the old stringing adage: restring your racket as many times per year as you play each week. Change your grips at least that often.

- Be sure to use new, lively balls every time you step onto the court. As balls get more and more use they become heavier and can put more pressure on your arm and shoulder. When you complete your game, give the balls to the club pro for his basket.

They Do More than Play Tennis

Whether it's swimming, biking, weight lifting, Yoga or something else, most super seniors do supplemental exercise to boost their on court performance and minimize their potential for injuries.

Fitness expert Corey Smith says that, "senior tennis players should be sure their fitness routine is all inclusive – cardio, strength, flexibility and balance. Without one, all the others become weak links on the court. Cardio fitness can be achieved by increasing your heart rate over a period of time. Choosing to cross train for your cardio, i.e. biking, swimming, elliptical, hiking; will only make you stronger on the court."

To increase and maintain your strength Corey suggests you consider hiring a personal trainer. "Meeting with a personal trainer with a tennis background can help you put together the appropriate exercises for your goals and limitations."

They Take Care of Their Bodies

Four hours of tennis, a three mile run and then three more sets after dinner was always a great start to my weekend. If I try that now, it finishes my week. Another thing that those ageless warriors down in Florida know is that they must treat their bodies with respect.

When your body talks to you, listen! I've learned that when my legs feel overly tight or my knees start to throb, it's time for a break. Plus, the occasional massage goes a long way towards helping me recover from my on and off court workouts. Massage promotes blood flow which in turn brings oxygen to our muscles and allows them to function more effectively.

Deep tissue massage is recommended for tennis players because it not only helps with the maintenance of our bones, muscles and tissues, it also promotes the healing of minor strains and sprains. To learn more about massage or to find a masseuse in your area go to massagetherapy.com.

They Watch What They Eat

Interestingly, none of the Villagers that I spoke to adhered to any of the highly publicized, new age, quick weight loss diets that we're bombarded with today. In fact, most of them ate what they wanted….. in moderation. The one common thread that I found was that they drank very little alcohol and every single one of them drank lots of water, on and off the court!

The benefits of water are highly publicized and most of us should drink more. Begin each morning with a tall glass of water and continue to drink as you move through your day. Take your body weight, divide it by two and you'll know how many ounces of water you need each day.

They Embrace Tennis…and Life

Over the years, I've interviewed hundreds of super seniors and found that the one ingredient they all possess is a positive attitude towards life. In fact, Dr. John F Murray says that, as we advance in years, "A healthy attitude is one of the key determinants to our quality of life."

Dr. Murray, a clinical and sport performance psychologist based in Palm Beach Florida, says that "the perspective one brings to any situation on and off the tennis court is even more important than the situation itself."

Players with a positive attitude view difficult shots as fun challenges. Losses inspire them to work harder to improve and pressure moments of a match are longed for rather than dreaded. As Billie Jean King said in the title of her recent book, "Pressure is a Privilege."

A positive attitude also means that you don't whine and complain, lose faith and argue when you can't move or hit shots as you did twenty years ago. Instead, smile and realize that every decade has its place in the life of a tennis player and that your goal is to be the best 50, 60 or 70 year-old player that you can be.

"Adopting a positive attitude", says Dr. Murray "begins with positive self-talk and the proper understanding of what it means to play tennis. If you approach the game with a narrow view that only the scoreboard matters and losing a match represents failure, then you're doomed from the get go. On the other hand, if you can look at your tennis as a challenge to get the most out of your game with what you have at the moment, you'll be forever inspired and excited to play." (More info: JohnFMurray.com)

A few words from some of Tim's Ageless Warriors:

Maggie Togliatti, age 66:   "I attribute my tennis longevity to maintaining physical health and restricting my tennis play to clay courts. I plan to play tennis as long as I am physically and mentally capable."

Beth Hollis, age 64: "I just love the game. Playing with confidence on a 3.5 level at sixty-four years of age is my accomplishment in tennis. Hopefully, I can continue to improve and will play as long as I am having fun."

Joe Ferrari, age 75: "I believe that staying active is the secret to sports longevity. I've gained friends, tennis knowledge and some trophies and I will continue to play as long as my health allows."

Mary Fischer, age 70: "Tennis really makes me feel good about myself. It's uplifting. My goal is to play competitive tennis until I am seventy-five years old (which isn't too far off). Then I plan to play until they ban me from the courts."

Pat Wiest, age 65: "I attribute my tennis longevity to having fun while I'm playing; getting "secret satisfaction" from executing a good shot, and knowing if I make an error, on another day, I can do better. Through tennis, I've accomplished a feeling of confidence and good health, along with gathering many friends and acquaintances along the way.

I feel that tennis is responsible for helping me develop from a very shy person to the position of team captain. I plan to continue playing for as long as I am able. True, the level of play may not remain the same, but hopefully the enjoyment of the game and the challenge will remain."

Tim doesn't see himself or The Villagers slowing down anytime in the near future. "We play tennis, paddle ball, softball, basketball and many other physical sports. In fact, we take pride in our physical well being which is a reflection of our positive outlook on life. Not enough can be said for being active. It will definitely enhance the quality of your life as you move into and through your senior years."

Yes, we may be getting older but that doesn't mean we have to get old. You do have a choice. Embrace your time on the court and view the tough times as challenges.

Tim Farwell and his friends at The Villages are living proof that, just as on the tennis court, the game of life can get more exciting in the third set.

Appendix A

USTA TENNIS RATING PROGRAM (NTRP)

1.0: You are a complete beginner

1.5: You have limited experience and are working primarily on getting the ball in play.

2.0: You lack court experience and your strokes need developing. You are familiar with the basic positions for singles and doubles play.

2.5: You are learning to judge where the ball is going, although your court coverage is limited. You can sustain a short rally of slow pace with other players of the same ability.

3.0: You are fairly consistent when hitting medium-paced shots, but are not comfortable with all strokes and lack execution when trying for directional control, depth, or power. Your most common doubles formation is one-up, one-back.

3.5: You have achieved improved stroke dependability with directional control on moderate shots, but need to develop depth and variety. You exhibit more aggressive net play, have improved court coverage and are developing teamwork in doubles.

4.0: You have dependable strokes, including directional control and depth on both forehand and backhand sides on moderate-paced shots. You can use lobs, overheads, approach shots and volleys with some success and occasionally force errors when serving. Rallies may be lost due to impatience. Teamwork in doubles is evident.

4.5: You have developed your use of power and spin and can handle pace. You have sound footwork, can control depth of shots, and attempt to vary game plan according to your opponents. You can hit first serves with power and accuracy and place the second serve. You tend to overhit on difficult shots. Aggressive net play is common in doubles.

5.0: You have good shot anticipation and frequently have an outstanding shot or attribute around which a game may be structured. You can regularly hit winners or force errors off of short balls and can put away volleys. You can successfully execute lobs, drop shots, half volleys, overhead smashes, and have good depth and spin on most second serves.

5.5: You have mastered power and/or consistency as a major weapon. You can vary strategies and styles of play in a competitive situation and hit dependable shots in a stress situation.

6.0 to 7.0: You have had intensive training for national tournament competition at the junior and collegiate levels and have obtained a sectional and/or national ranking.

7.0: You are a world-class player.

(More info: usta.com)

Appendix B

General Responsibilities of Each Player

The Server:

1. Get your first serve in. Strive for a 70 % percentage. Studies show that the serving team wins the point 75% of the time when the first serve goes in.

2. Hit the majority of your serves at the "T" or into the receiver's body.

3. Follow both serves to the net and take control of the point.

The Server's Partner:

1. Protect your alley.

2. Anticipate and cover all lobs that you can hit in the air on your side of the court.

3. Be aggressive. Fake or poach on every ball that crosses the net.

The Receiver:

1. Get the return of serve back in play. A missed return is just as bad as a double fault. Even the worst return makes your opponents hit the ball.

2. Keep your return away from the net man. Aim low at the server's feet if he's coming in, cross-court and deep if he stays back.

3. Keep the server's partner under control by occasionally hitting down the alley and lobbing over him.

4. If facing a second serve shift into attack mode. Return cross-court and attack the net.

The Receiver's Partner:

1. Stand facing the opposing net player.

2. Determine as soon as possible what type of return your partner has hit. Do this by keeping your eyes glues to the server's partner.

If the return goes to the net player shift to the center and get ready to react. If it goes past the net player low to the oncoming server, move in. If the server stays back and the return goes cross-court, move in and look to poach.

Appendix C

Setting Up Your Battlefield

Formation	Advantages	Disadvantages
Both Players Up	Puts tremendous pressure on your opponents. Easier to put the ball away from the net position.	Both players must have excellent volley, overhead, movement and anticipation skills. The vulnerable area in this formation is a deep lob to the backcourt.
One Up, One Back	Best for lower level players as it allows one player to cover the net and the other to patrol the backcourt. Also can be effective if one player has exceptionally strong groundstrokes.	The vulnerable area of this setup is the huge hole down the center of the court. Plus, against an opposing team that has both players up, the single "up" player becomes a sitting duck.
Both Players Back	A defensive position that makes it harder for opponents to end the point. Through the clever use of lobs and drives, you can force your opponents to hit a lot of balls and test their patience.	Backcourt players will have to cover more territory as well as work harder generating groundstrokes. The vulnerable areas are: drop volleys as well as angled shots.

Appendix D

The Tiebreaker

I've lost count of the number of times I've seen players befuddled as to how to play a tiebreaker. Well, let the confusion end. Here's how it's done.

1. At six games all, a 12 point tiebreaker will be played to determine the set.

2. The team that wins seven points first, with a margin of two points, wins the set.

3. To start, the player whose turn it is to serve next will serve one point to the deuce court.

4. The player on the opposing team then due to serve will serve two points, beginning on the ad side

5. The next player in sequence serves two points and so on until one team reaches seven points with a margin of two.

6. Teams switch sides every six points.

7. Once the tiebreaker is completed the score of the set is recorded for the winner as 7-6.

8. The team that received the first point of the tiebreaker begins serving the next set.

The Coman Tiebreaker

In recent years, the USTA has adopted what's known as the Coman Tiebreaker to decide sets or as a third set match tiebreaker. In the Coman Tiebreaker, teams will play the first to win ten points with a margin of two. The serving rotation is exactly the same as the twelve point tiebreaker with the following exception:

Players will switch sides after point 1, 5, 9, 13, 17 ...and the last point.

By having teams switch sides more frequently, the elements (wind and sun) will be more evenly distributed between the two teams as opposed to the traditional format where teams play six consecutive points before changing ends. Plus, the server will always serve from the same end of the court, rather than having to serve from both ends.

Select References

A special thanks to all of the fabulous teaching professionals who took time out of their busy schedules to contribute drills and tips for this book.

Jorge Capestany & Luke Jensen: tennisdrills.tv

Brent Abel: webtennis.net

Jeff Greenwald: mentaledge.net

Ken Dehart: kendehart10s.com

Pat Etcheberry: etcheberryexperience.com

Corey Smith: csmith@sportsplexbethel.com

Credits

Words from the Wise reprinted from:

Tennis Magazine: Ajay Pant, Rick Macci, Jimmy Pitkanan, Paula Scheb, Mike O'Connell, Will Hoag, Dave Hagler

Tennis.com: Brad Gilbert, Paul Annacone, Doug Spreen

Tennis Life Magazine: Nick Bollettieri

TennisOne.com: Mark Fairchilds

Index

Be Empowered!

More Breakthrough Books from Mansion Grove House

MAKING WEIGHT CONTROL SECOND NATURE

A leading dietitian's unique journey from overweight to permanent weight control, naturally. Join in! Susan inspires us with her personal weight control triumph as well as her professional expertise. David Katz, Director, Prevention Research Center, Yale University says "Being thin and healthy, eating what you like yet liking yourself, and controlling your weight without fixating on it for the rest of your life are not about natural gifts, but about the gift of knowing how. That's a gift you can give yourself."
ISBN-13 9781932421194

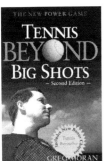

TENNIS BEYOND BIG SHOTS

Win BIG with Small Changes! A book for every tennis enthusiast. Tennis Beyond Big Shots presents a bold back-to-the-future approach. A new game that moves away from power and big shots yet is more lethal to opponents than any booming serve. Award winning Pro and Director of Tennis at The Four Seasons Racquet Club, Wilton, CT, Greg enthusiastically teaches top ranked players, working warriors as well as eager beginners. A prolific contributing writer for leading tennis magazines, he has also appeared on television to share his strategies for winning, playing longer and enjoying more.
ISBN-13 9781932421170

COACHING YOUR TENNIS CHAMPION

Want new games to get your 8-year old excited about tennis? No problem. David's Coaching Your Tennis Champion uses the new QuickStart Tennis format and lays out progressive game plans organized day-by-day and for each age group. Simply turn to the appropriate page..voila! you have your bright new idea for Game of the Day! You will love it! Your juniors will adore it! Big time-saver for coaches. Fun know-how for parents!
ISBN-13 9781932421156

AMERICAN DOUBLES

A close-up view that is intriguing, exciting and impossible to put down. Many fans and journalists lament the state of American tennis, wondering when the next great players will hit the scene. What the critics may not realize is that Americans have dominated the doubles scene for decades and the future looks bright.
ISBN-13 9781932421163

RAISING BIG SMILING TENNIS KIDS

Whether you are a tennis playing parent or a parent curious about tennis, this book will empower you to raise kids who swing the tennis racket with as much aplomb as their happy smiles. The best age to get your kid started in tennis. How to motivate kids to go back, practice after practice. When to focus exclusively on tennis. Save on lessons, find scholarships and sponsors. How to pursue a career in professional tennis. Gain insight into tennis organizations and agents. Have fun along the way at the best tennis camps and resort.

ISBN-13 9781932421118

GOLF GUIDE FOR PARENTS AND PLAYERS

Jack Nicklaus acclaimed guide unveils the secrets of success for junior and college golf, the professional tour and beyond. Golf pros Jacqui and Johnny, offer exclusive guidance and new ideas on: How to motivate kids to go back, practice after practice. When to focus exclusively on golf. Save on lessons, find scholar-ships and sponsors. How to pursue college golf and a career in professional golf. Gain insight into golf organizations and agents. Have fun along the way at the best golf camps and resorts.

ISBN-13 9781932421149

RAISING BIG SMILING SQUASH KIDS

Stanford University recently added Squash to its athletics, joining Yale and Cornell. Forbes magazine rates Squash as the number one sport for fitness. With courts and college programs springing up across the country. Richard Millman, world-class coach and Georgetta Morque, a prolific sportswriter, offer a complete road-map for parents, professionals and kids. The best age to get started in squash; how to motivate kids; the road to top colleges; and attractive career options. Plus: cultivating friendships, character building and achieving a lifetime of fitness.

ISBN 1932421432

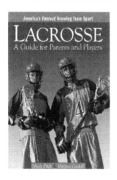

LACROSSE: A GUIDE FOR PARENTS AND PLAYERS

Lacrosse is America's fastest growing team sport. Action-packed and fun, lacrosse is a game anyone can play — the big and small, boys and girls. Lacrosse offers a positive outlet, a place to fit in at school, motivation to excel, and opportunities for team travel. Whether your kid is 8 or 18, experienced or just starting, this book is the complete guide to all that lacrosse has to offer. Empower yourself with practical answers and unique ideas, whether you are new to lacrosse or once were a player. Make lacrosse an exhilarating part of your family life.

ISBN 1932421076

Available Worldwide

Tennis Doubles Beyond Big Shots
Companion Video

50-minutes of exclusive instruction from top teaching professionals

❖ Luke Jensen, Grand Slam Tennis Doubles Champion, ESPN TV Analyst

❖ Jorge Capestany, Master Tennis Professional

❖ Brent Abel, Tennis Teaching Professional

❖ Jeff Greenwald, Sports Psychologist

❖ Corey Smith, Fitness Instructor

❖ Host: Greg Moran

<u>Free to our readers</u>! _Sponsored by_:

6922428R00123

Printed in Great Britain
by Amazon.co.uk, Ltd.,
Marston Gate.